Resisting Bondage in Indian Ocean Africa and Asia

Resisting Bondage in Indian Ocean Africa and Asia is the companion volume to *Slavery and Resistance in Africa and Asia* which was published by Routledge in 2005. This second volume, as implied by the title, recognizes the complexity of forms of bondage in the Indian Ocean world – incorporating regions running from East Africa to the Middle East, to South and Southeast Asia to the Far East – and of resistance to them.

Slavery, in the conventional sense of the word, was in the region covered one of many, often overlapping, forms of unfree labour that included, in addition, various types of forced or *corvée* labour, debt bondage and indentured or contract labour. This volume examines resistance to forms of bondage in a variety of precolonial, colonial and postcolonial regimes, from revolt against slavery in South Africa, to resistance to colonial forced labour schemes in Somalia, the Indian Ocean islands of Mayotta and Madagascar, India, Indonesia and Indochina, and the fight of Aborigines for human rights on the cattle ranches of Northern Australia.

Just as the companion volume *Slavery and Resistance in Africa and Asia* revealed that reactions to slavery in Africa and Asia were far more complex than the conventional historical emphasis on forms of 'revolt' implies, this collection of essays reveals an unexpectedly wide range of often very subtle forms of resistance to a variety of repressive labour regimes in the Indian Ocean world. In so doing, it will appeal to all those interested in exploring the wider debate over the structure of unfree labour regimes and resistance to them.

Edward A. Alpers is Professor of History at the University of California, Los Angeles, USA. **Gwyn Campbell** is Canada Research Chair in Indian Ocean World History in the Department of History, McGill University, Canada. **Michael Salman** is an Associate Professor of History at the University of California at Los Angeles.

Routledge studies in slave and post-slave societies and cultures
Edited by Gad Heuman

1 **Abolition and its Aftermath in Indian Ocean Africa and Asia**
Edited by Gwyn Campbell

2 **Resisting Bondage in Indian Ocean Africa and Asia**
Edited by Edward A. Alpers, Gwyn Campbell and Michael Salman

Previous titles to appear in Routledge studies in slave and post-slave societies and cultures include:

The Structure of Slavery in Indian Ocean Africa and Asia
Edited by Gwyn Campbell

Representing the Body of the Slave
Edited by Thomas Wiedemann and Jane Gardner

Rethinking the African Diaspora
The making of a Black Atlantic world in the Bight of Benin and Brazil
Edited by Kristin Mann and Edna G. Bay

After Slavery
Emancipation and its discontents
Edited by Howard Temperley

From Slavery to Emancipation in the Atlantic World
Edited by Sylvia R. Frey and Betty Wood

Slavery and Colonial Rule in Africa
Edited by Suzanne Miers and Martin A. Klein

Classical Slavery
Edited by M. I. Finley

Popular Politics and British Anti-Slavery
The mobilisation of public opinion against the slave trade, 1787–1807
J. R. Oldfield

Routes to Slavery
Direction, ethnicity and mortality in the transatlantic slave trade
Edited by David Eltis and David Richardson

Resisting Bondage in Indian Ocean Africa and Asia

Edited by Edward A. Alpers,
Gwyn Campbell and Michael Salman

Routledge
Taylor & Francis Group

LONDON AND NEW YORK

First published 2007
by Routledge
2 Park Square, Milton Park, Abingdon, Oxon OX14 4RN

Simultaneously published in the USA and Canada
by Routledge
711 Third Avenue, New York, NY 10017

Routledge is an imprint of the Taylor & Francis Group, an informa business

First issued in paperback 2016

Typeset in Garamond by Wearset Ltd, Boldon, Tyne and Wear
Printed and bound in Great Britain by TJI Digital, Padstow, Cornwall

British Library Cataloguing in Publication Data
A catalogue record for this book is available from the British Library

Library of Congress Cataloging in Publication Data
A catalog record for this book has been requested

ISBN13: 978–0–415–77151–1 (hbk)
ISBN13: 978–1–138–98528–5 (pbk)

Contents

Notes on contributors   ix

1   Introduction: resisting bondage in the Indian Ocean
    world   1
    GWYN CAMPBELL, EDWARD A. ALPERS AND
    MICHAEL SALMAN

2   Revolt in Cape Colony slave society   10
    NIGEL WORDEN

3   Unfree labour, forced labour and resistance among the
    Zigula of the Lower Juba   24
    FRANCESCA DECLICH

4   Forced labour and the 1856 revolt on Mayotta   40
    ISABELLE DENIS

5   Unfree labour, slavery and protest in imperial
    Madagascar   49
    GWYN CAMPBELL

6   Forced labour in Madagascar under Vichy, 1940–42:
    autarky, forced labour and resistance on the
    'Red Island'   60
    ERIC JENNINGS

7   Sugar and servility: themes of forced labour, resistance
    and accommodation in mid-nineteenth-century Java   69
    G. ROGER KNIGHT

8   Forced labourers and their resistance in Java under
     Japanese military rule, 1942–45   82
     SHIGERU SATO

9   'Unfree' labour on the cattle stations of Northern
     Australia, the tea gardens of Assam and the rubber
     plantations of Indo-China, 1920–50   96
     ROBERT CASTLE, JAMES HAGAN AND
     ANDREW WELLS

     Index   114

Contributors

Edward A. Alpers is Professor of History at the University of California, Los Angeles. He has also taught at the Universities of Dar es Salaam, Tanzania and the Somali National University, Lafoole. In 1994 he served as President of the African Studies Association. Alpers has published widely on the history of East Africa and the Indian Ocean. His major publications include *Ivory and Slaves in East Central Africa* (London: Heinemann/Berkeley: University of California Press, 1975) and co-edited volumes on *Walter Rodney: Revolutionary and Scholar* (Los Angeles: Center for Afro-American Stduies, UCLA, 1982); *Africa and the West: A Documentary History of the Slave Trade to Independence* (Phoenix: Oryx, 2001); *History, Memory and Identity* (Port Louis: Nelson Mandela Centre for African Culture and University of Mauritius, 2001); *Sidis and Scholars: Essays on African Indians* (Noida: Rainbow Publishers, 2004); *Slavery and Resistance in Africa and Asia* (London: Routledge, 2005); and *Slave Routes and Oral Tradition in Southeastern Africa* (Maputo: Filsom, 2005). His current research focuses on the African Diaspora in the Indian Ocean.

Gwyn Campbell is Canada Research Chair in Indian Ocean World History in the Department of History, McGill University. His most recent publications include *An Economic History of Imperial Madagascar, 1750–1895: The Rise and Fall of an Island Empire* (Cambridge: Cambridge University Press, 2005); editor, *Abolition and Its Aftermath in Indian Ocean Africa and* Asia (London: Routledge, 2005); co-editor (with Edward A. Alpers and Michael Salman), *Slavery and Resistance in Africa and Asia* (London: Routledge, 2005); co-editor (with Suzanne Miers and Joseph C. Miller), *Women in Western Systems of Slavery* – special edition of *Slavery & Abolition* 26.2 (2005); and editor, *The Structure of Slavery in Indian Ocean Africa and Asia* (London: Frank Cass, 2004). He is currently completing *Africa and the Indian Ocean World from Early Times to 1900* – to appear in the new *Cambridge Economic History of Africa* series, and is undertaking research into slavery and diaspora in the Indian Ocean World and the foundations of the Indian Ocean world global economy.

Robert Castle is Deputy Vice-Chancellor (Academic) and Professor of Economics at the University of Wollongong. His research interests are in labour, employment and international economic institutions. He is the author of *Evolution of Economic Ideas and Labour Economics* (Oxford University Press) and also edited *Unemployment in the Eighties and Work, Leisure and Technology* (Longmans). He has contributed to a major child labour study for the government of Vietnam.

Francesca Declich, a social anthropologist, studied at the Istituto Universitario Orientale di Napoli and the London School of Economics and spent time as a post-doctoral researcher at SOAS in London. She is now a researcher and lecturer at the University of Urbino, Italy. Her major fieldwork has been in southern Somalia and Tanzania. She has written *The Somali Bantu. Ethnogenesis and* mviko *rituals* (Rome, 2002), and published a number of edited books and journal articles.

Isabelle Denis is currently completing her doctoratal thesis, 'Intérêts de la France dans l'océan indien, presence militaire à Mayotte, 1841–1945' at the University of the Sorbonne, Paris. She obtained a DEA from the University of the Sorbonne, Paris IV (1991), a masters degree from the University of Orléans (1990). Her publications include 'Des marins fantassins de marine du XIXè siècle aux gendarmes du XXè siècle, essai d'étude prosopographique comparative' in S. Mohamed-Gaillard and M. Romo-Navarette (eds.), *Des Français outre mer* (Paris: Presses Univeristaires de la Sorbonne, 2004), 'l'évolution du statut de Mayotte: une relation particulière avec la métropole,' AMAROM 24 (2005) and 'les lieux de mémoire à Mayotte,' Outremer (2006).

James Hagan is Emeritus Professor of History and Professorial Fellow at the University of Wollongong. He has written and edited many books, including *A History of the Australian Council of Trade Unions (1981)* and (with Ken Turner) *A History of the Labour Party in New South Wales* (1901). With Rob Castle and Andrew Wells he has published several articles on native labour in India, Malaya, Vietnam and Australia. He is currently working with them on a project which compares the employment of Aboriginal and coolie labour in the beef, tea, rubber and sugar industries, from about 1860 to 1940.

Eric Jennings is Associate Professor of History at the University of Toronto. He is the author of *Vichy in the Tropics: Petain's National Revolution in Madagascar, Guadeloupe, and Indochina, 1940–44* (Stanford: Stanford University Press, 2001), co-editor with Jacques Cantier of *L'Empire colonial sous Vichy* (Paris: Odile Jacob, 2004), *Curing the Colonizers: Hydrotherapy, Climatology and French Colonial Spas* (Durham, NC: Duke University Press, 2006), and the author of numerous articles and chapters.

G. Roger Knight is Associate Professor of History at the University of Adelaide and researches the social and economic history of colonial Indonesia. His most recent publications include his several contributions to Ulbe Bosma, Juan Giusti and G. Roger Knight (eds), *Sugarlandia Revisited: Sugar and Colonialism in Asia and the Americas, 1800–1940*, with a preface by Sydney Mintz (London: Berghahn Publishers, 2006) and 'A Precocious Appetite: Industrial Agriculture and the Fertiliser Revolution in Java's Colonial Cane Fields, *c*.1880–1914', *The Journal of Southeast Asian Studies*, 37. 1 (2006). He is at present completing a book provisionally entitled *Steam, Steel and Cane: Sugar's Singular Trajectory in Colonial Java*.

Michael Salman is an Associate Professor of History at the University of California at Los Angeles, with interdisciplinary interests in the history of the Philippines and Southeast Asia, American colonialism and empire, slavery and abolition, and the epistemological problems of comparative studies. He is author of *The Embarrassment of Slavery: Controversies over Bondage and Nationalism in the American Colonial Philippines* (University of California Press, 2001 and 2003; Ateneo de Manila University Press, 2001) and essays on American empire, the epistemology of Southeast Asian studies, and historiography of the Philippines.

Shigeru Sato teaches in the School of Humanities and Social Science, The University of Newcastle, Australia. He has published extensively on occupation, collaboration and resistance in Asia during the Second World War, and the war's impact on the peasantry in Indonesia. He currently works as an editor of and a contributor to *The Encyclopaedia of Indonesia in the Pacific War* that is being prepared by the Netherlands Institute for War Documentation.

Andrew Wells is Professor of Comparative History and Dean of Arts at the University of Wollongong. He has published widely on economic labour and social history, including *Constructing Capitalism*, *A History of Wollongong*, and *Japanese/Australian Labour Relations* both edited with Jim Hagan. He is currently researching the commodification of colonial labour, Asian ports and digital archives.

Nigel Worden, Professor of Historical Studies at the University of Cape Town, has published extensively on slavery and post-emancipation society in the Cape Colony. His books include *Slavery in Dutch South Africa* (Cambridge: Cambridge University Press, 1985) and he edited, with Clifton Crias, *Breaking the Chains: Slavery and its Legacy in the Nineteenth-century Cape Colony* (Johannesburg: Witwatersrand University Press, 1994). He is currently working on the formation of social identities in VOC Cape Town.

1 Introduction

Resisting bondage in the Indian Ocean world

Gwyn Campbell, Edward A. Alpers and Michael Salman

Background

This volume presents a number of examples of resistance in the Indian Ocean world (IOW) from South Africa to the Indian Ocean islands of Mayotta and Madagascar, to India, Australia, Java and Indochina. Bondage in the IOW assumed a multiplicity of often overlapping forms that varied according to region and inevitably changed over time. They ranged from permanent chattel slavery, characteristic of 'closed' slave systems of the Far East and European-run plantations on the Mascarene islands in the eighteenth and nineteenth centuries, to multiple and flexible forms of servility, such as existed in many 'open' slave systems in Africa and Southeast Asia, in which changes in status from free to servile and vice versa were often possible. At the same time, the gender and age profile of servile labour in the IOW varied enormously over time and according to region and the system of bondage. Thus whereas adult males were most in demand on the Mascarenes plantations, females and children were often the most sought after forms of servile labour in traditional forms of bondage in indigenous IOW societies. Again, whereas Buddhism, Hinduism and Christianity had relatively little impact upon the attitude of slave-owners subscribing to those faiths towards their slaves, Islam did affect many Muslim slave-owners' attitudes to their slaves; for example, most children of a Muslim master and a female slave were automatically granted freedom, as was their mother upon the death of the father.

At the same time, as outlined in a number of recent works, most IOW societies were traditionally characterized by hierarchical social structures with a number of horizontal divisions of status, each of which involved obligatory duties to those of superior status, and obligations to those of inferior status. Moreover, gradations of hierarchy also characterized the internal structure of each of the major status markers. Thus some slaves were of superior status to others, and slave status often overlapped with other forms of servitude. For instance, in nineteenth-century Imperial Madagascar, virtually the entire non-elite population was subjected to some degree of unfree labour, either as slaves or as victims of *fanompoana* (unremunerated forced labour) for the Merina state and ruling elite.[1] This agitates against the often simplistic picture of resistance against servitude, and it is sometimes difficult to discern resistance against systems of unfree labour per se from other sentiments of animosity; inter-status, inter-ethnic; anti-state; anti-imperial etc.[2]

These complex structures of traditional systems of servile labour in the IOW inevitably affected the impact of pro-abolitionist forces and colonialism in the nineteenth and twentieth centuries, as G. Roger Knight and Francesca Declich, amongst others, point out.[3] Of notable importance in terms of resistance to servitude under colonialism was the definition applied by Western powers to 'slavery' in the IOW, the pace of emancipation of 'slaves', and the overlap between forced labour regimes imposed by the colonial power and those that existed in pre-colonial times.

Resistance

A number of studies highlight the alleged passivity of servile labour in the IOW. In part this has been ascribed to traditional religious and ideological values that stressed obedience to those in positions of power, in part – notably by colonial authorities – to the benign nature of servitude. However, as outlined above, it is clear that the forms of servitude were more complex than is often assumed, and that forms of resistance to them were expressed in manifest, often subtle ways. Agency in systems of servitude was not, as traditionally has often been over-simplistically portrayed, an issue of uprisings and revolt in which the participants were predominantly adult males. Rather, resistance assumed many different forms that were engaged in by female and child as well as by adult male bondspeople.

Revolt

While attacks on overseers and others in lower positions of authority were relatively frequent in some locales, recorded instances of outright revolt or rebellion in the IOW are rare compared with those that occurred in the Americas. The 'Zanj' revolt in ninth-century Iraq was for long held up as a prime example of a slave revolt in the IOW, but it is now evident that the revolt was orchestrated and led by free people with a local agenda, and that those 'Zanj' who were involved were not, as originally thought, from East Africa, but rather from Ethiopia.

However, several instances of slave revolt in the IOW are cited in this volume. The greatest possibility for revolt was in economies, such as plantations, that required large numbers of servile workers. This was the background to the 1856 revolt on Mayotta, analysed by Isabelle Denis. Mayotta was taken over by the French in 1843 and slavery abolished there in 1847, a year before it was abolished in other French colonial possessions, largely because of the pro-abolitionist sentiments of the imperial officers on neighbouring Réunion, which largely administered Mayotta. However, the establishment there of a plantation economy dependent upon cheap labour resulted in a number of measures that ensured the continuation of forced labour. The ex-slave population was obliged to work for planters, 'engagés' were recruited from East Africa and in the early 1850s, when such supplies proved insufficient, local Comorians judged to be landless were classified as 'vagabonds' and could be forced into plantation work. However, when legislation governing contracts for hired workers was ignored by French planters, and the authorities rejected complaints from workers that planters were ill-treating them, refusing to pay wages and otherwise breaking contract clauses, a revolt erupted from March to May 1856 involving up to 600 insurgents, almost all male, that was finally suppressed by military force.[4]

South Africa did not possess plantations, but Nigel Worden notes that several types of 'rebellion' occurred amongst bondspeople there.[5] From 1799 to 1803 hundreds of Khoi and San forced farm labourers joined Xhosa bands to attack settler farms before being defeated by the British military. Again, following abolition of the slave trade in 1808 several hundred slaves attempted to march on Cape Town to demand the emancipation that had been granted slaves in Britain. Another smaller rebellion in 1825 similarly followed an 1823 act enforcing better slave conditions and the right of slaves to protest legally against ill-treatment. Both involved mainly male slaves and both were quickly suppressed. The final revolt was in 1850–53 when Khoi and ex-slave rebels again united with the Xhosa to attack white colonists. As Worden underlines, all involved different types of bonded workers – indicating a broad sharing of experience and values by different forms of servile labour.

Knight, in his contribution on the *Cultuurstelsel* system practised in Java from the 1830s to 1880s, notes the surprising absence of New World-style revolt in an island that by mid-century was the second largest sugar cane producer after Cuba, and where sugar production depended largely on forced labour.[6] This absence of revolt he ascribes to peasant familiarity with a variety of traditional forms of servile labour to which the Dutch corvée system only added another layer, and the dependence of the Dutch upon the cooperation of the Javanese elite for access to labour – which led to the corvée they imposed being relatively light. Consequently, sugar production's demand for land and labour did not impact negatively on peasant subsistence. Rather, Knight concludes, the *Cultuurstelsel* system enabled most peasants to continue working the land for subsistence purposes, and may even have brought them additional income. Indeed, cane-burning, often considered a classic form of protest, occurred rarely until the late nineteenth century and may well have been a reflection of inter-worker and inter-landlord animosity more than hostility to the *Cultuurstelsel* per se.

Shigeru Sato's contribution on the *romusha* forced labour regime imposed on the Javanese during the 1942–45 Japanese occupation notes a similar lack of revolt by workers, which he attributes to the Japanese presence being even less oppressive than that of the Dutch.[7] *Romusha* workers were not involved in the most serious revolts; one in April–July 1944 involving farmers protesting against the compulsory delivery of rice to the government, during which the army shot hundreds of rioters but subsequently lifted their monopoly over local rice production; and two swiftly and bloodily suppressed revolts in February 1944 and February 1945 that were apparently nationalist reactions to the slowness of the Japanese to implement their pledge, issued upon 'liberating' the Javanese from Dutch rule, that they would grant independence to the Javanese.

The Javanese case studies contrast strongly with the forced labour imposed by the state, both pre-colonial and colonial, in Madagascar – the subject of papers by Gwyn Campbell and Eric Jennings[8] – which became so onerous that it threatened the self-sufficiency of the peasant and led to serious uprisings; one in 1840s sabotaged the Merina attempt to forge an industrial revolution in Madagascar, another in the 1880s by African slaves 'liberated' into forced labour in 1877 gravely threatened gold production in northwest Madagascar.

Community solidarity

Some defied externally imposed forced labour through community solidarity, as Declich notes for some Zigula communities in the Lower Juba River region of southern Somalia under Italian rule during the inter-war years. The descendants of free farmers and former WaGosha runaway slaves, the Zigula considered five days a week of forced labour for Italian farmer settlers or for public works to be tantamount to the slavery from which many of their parents had previously fled. Frequently, men summoned to work hid in the nearby bush when soldiers came to escort them to settler farms, but such tactics were increasingly met by violence to their wives or the taking of elders in their place. More successful was resistance organized by village leaders. While most leaders complied, at least partially, with the administration's orders and sent off workers, some leaders, assured of entire communal solidarity, simply refused – and with apparent success. Moreover, some such communities established common links to reinforce their opposition to the imposition of forced labour.

Ideology

As noted above, the alleged passivity of servile labour in the IOW has often been ascribed to traditional religious and ideological values that stressed obedience to those in positions of power. However, there were instances in which servile labour attempted to thwart the power structure through allegiance to alternative, sometimes potentially revolutionary ideologies. Such was the case from 1829 to 1861 in Imperial Madagascar when slaves formed possibly the majority of Christian proselytes. Indeed, it was in large part due to a realization of the revolutionary potential of a Christian slave body that the Merina Court first banned slave access to Christian chapels and education, and in 1835 made Christianity treasonable. Ironically, when the ban on Christianity was lifted in 1862, it was the new wave of missionaries from the London Missionary Society, rather than the Merina authorities, that effectively barred slave access to positions of control within the church. Slaves subsequently attempted to integrate into Malagasy ancestral traditions, through creating or claiming 'ancestral tombs' and through possession cults in which they represented ancestral sovereigns and in some cases helped shape major historical events.[9]

Also, Robert Castle, Jim Hagan and Andrew Wells note that in French Indochina in the 1930s, rubber plantation workers were increasingly won over by Communist and Socialist ideology. They started to form links with revolutionary groups in the towns and in at least one case formed a union – although its leaders were arrested and imprisoned.[10]

Petitioning

One form of protest by servile labourers was petitioning, although this invariably appears to have failed. For instance, Knight notes that in October 1842, during the early phase of the *Cultuurstelsel* system in Java, some 600 peasants in the north coast town of Pekalongan protested about inadequate remuneration to the Dutch Resident who, however, persuaded them to disperse and had the organizers punished.[11] Similar protests against state-imposed forced labour in Imperial Madagascar were crushed with great ruthlessness.[12]

Declich notes that petitioning also occurred in Italian Somaliland, less against forced labour per se than against aspects of it. She cites one case in which from 800 to 900 men and women marched to demand of the regional Italian commissioner that accommodation be built on the concessions for wives to accompany drafted workers. The commissioner made vague promises to ameliorate the situation, but the protest appears to have died down after he summoned soldiers to arrest and hold the leader in jail for nine days. The 1930s depression appears to have been key to the politicization and growth in organizational strength of servile workers. At Phu-rieng in French Indochina in January 1930, a major demonstration by indentured rubber plantation labourers demanding better conditions of work was similarly suppressed by troops, and its leaders imprisoned.[13] Also, in Northern Australia in the 1920s, Aboriginal organizations began to develop in urban areas and helped to push the rights of rural workers on to the political agenda.

Negative forms of resistance

Women subject to slavery and other systems of servitude commonly took anti-conception measures, induced miscarriages or practised abortion and infanticide in a complex reaction to forced labour systems.[14] Similar 'negative' forms of resistance included self-mutilation, practised on the rubber plantations of colonial Vietnam,[15] and in Imperial Madagascar as a means by which recruits attempted to escape the Merina army.[16] Other negative forms of 'resistance' included, in Imperial Madagascar, the abandonment of crafts by artisans subjected to forced labour.[17]

Flight

Flight was a ubiquitous form of resistance to forced labour. Nigel Worden analyses the largely small-scale, day-to-day resistance of bondspeople in Cape Colony prior to 1833 where the economy, both urban and rural, was largely dependent on slave labour, both locally enslaved Khoi and San, and some 60,000 slaves imported between 1658 and 1807 from East Africa, Madagascar and Asia.[18] These formed a considerable proportion, sometimes a majority, of the total population of the Cape. However, farms were small-scale holdings and nowhere were slave-owners heavily outnumbered by slaves. There were no slave revolts such as characterized some of the American plantation economies. Other forms of resistance thus predominated. The most obvious was maroonage in which, at times, up to eight per cent of urban slaves engaged. An essentially individual affair, the incidence of slave flight to the unguarded interior of the Cape was high, notably amongst foreign-born male slaves. Some merely wished to escape harvest work, and returned before winter set in, but other fugitives forged permanent bands, from nearby Table Mountain to far into the interior. Yet others managed to escape as stowaways on passing ships. Again, from the 1830s, many Khoi and slaves similarly fled farms, some to form brigand bands, others to found agricultural settlements.

Campbell considers flight to have been the most common reaction to forced labour in nineteenth-century Madagascar where maroon communities, forged of political and religious dissidents as well as of refugees from forced labour, in combination with Sakalava and Bara opponents of Merina imperialism, were key components in the eventual collapse of the Merina Empire. Jennings notes that evasion, through hiding from recruiters, migration and flight were characteristic of the Vichy regime's attempts to impose massive forced labour in Madagascar from 1940 to 1942.[19]

In colonial Java, flight was also a common reaction of workers to forced labour in the early stages of the *Cultuurstelsel* sugar system. Knight notes that this may well have resulted in communities of 'vagabonds', some of whom were drawn back temporarily into sugar production as hired hands. However, most refugees fled to the expanding frontier of wet-rice agriculture in east-central Java, in what may have been less a protest against *Cultuurstelsel* than a reflection of traditional peasant mobility. Later, under Japanese occupation, flight from forced labour was again common, although it is debatable whether this was a reaction to harsh working conditions or opportunism as workers were most likely to flee after having received advance wages – a procedure the Japanese adopted in order to attract labour. The lack of supervision facilitated such flight. However, many refugees suffered illness and high mortality rates due less to the Japanese than to penury and disease resulting from the war conditions.

Again, for Italian Somaliland, Declich notes that flight from forced labour was a common, mostly individual reaction, refugees fleeing either to towns or to the protection of pastoral communities. Castle, Hagan and Wells note that from 1925 to 1935, over 10,000 coolies fled (desertion rates were as high as 10 per cent per annum) from rubber plantations in French Indochina despite police and militia hunts for fugitives and heavy punishment for those caught. They also underline that Aborigines in servile labour on the cattle ranches of Northern Australia would, despite the deterrent of the distances involved and employer and police harassment, often indulge in 'walkabouts' as maroonage was termed there, notably immediately following the rainy season when game and edible plants and fruit were relatively abundant.

Go-slows and strikes

Commonly, those in the IOW subject to systems of forced labour manifested resistance through go-slow tactics. Thus Knight notes that colonial records in nineteenth-century Java frequently refer to poor worker turnout and cultivation techniques – for which village headmen supervisors were often punished. However, such 'resistance' declined as the *Cultuurstelsel* matured. By contrast, Sato notes that low worker turnout (as low as 40 per cent in some instances) and go-slows increased in Java under the Japanese occupation as conditions steadily worsened prior to the end of the Second World War. Some workers organized protests in which an entire labour unit slackened the pace of their work so that the tasks of a particular day could not be accomplished.

Because of internecine disputes and repressive measures by the authorities, it was difficult for servile groups of workers to strike. However, the slave porters of Imperial Madagascar were notorious not only for go-slows but also for the successful use of strike tactics to ameliorate their conditions of work.[20] Also, the 1918 strike by over 200,000 tea-plantation workers in the Chargola and Surma Valleys of Assam, while repressed with force, led by 1925 to a repeal of the last laws treating a breach of indenture as a criminal offence. From 1930 to 1939, there were at least a further 115 strikes on the tea plantations of Assam, most in favour of higher wages, but none succeeded.[21] In 1947 and 1950, Aborigines employed in servile conditions on cattle ranches in Northern Australia also went on strike in Darwin in what was eventually a successful bid for better wages and working conditions.

Revenge

Revenge against collaborators with powers that imposed forced labour regimes also appears to have been common. Thus Declich notes for Italian Somaliland that revenge was sometimes taken on local chiefs who were strongly identified with, and profited from, the implementation of the forced labour system and the punishment of those who resisted it. Many spells are said to have been cast against one such man, Mze Maiange, who is said to have died after a sequence of serious illnesses that people ascribe to his abuse of the people. Castle, Hagan and Wells note that attacks on tea-plantation supervisors in colonial Assam were also frequent and that in 1930 rebels killed Hervé Bazin, owner of the largest recruitment agency in French Indochina.

However, revenge appears to have been more widespread in the immediate aftermath of the end of forced labour systems. Indeed, Sato writes that in Java the *romusha* only expressed open discontent after the Japanese capitulation when, freed from forced labour, they vented their anger on the local Javanese authorities and Chinese rice dealers who had profited from black-marketeering and collaboration with the occupation forces.

Accommodation

Possibly the most effective forms of resistance were practised by workers who formed an inter-dependency with the systems of forced labour in which they worked. For example, Campbell writes that in Imperial Madagascar slaves with the ability to pay the price of their redemption often chose to remain a slave, and rather use additional savings to purchase another slave whom they might use as a substitute for their own labour, because *fanompoana* – unremunerated forced labour for 'free' subjects – was universally regarded as more exploitative than slavery. Again, Knight notes that factory-cane haulers in Java who transported the cane from the fields to the factories on buffalo-hauled carts were crucial to the system because the cane needed to be processed as soon after cutting as possible. By mid-century, many haulers were able to take advantage of dependence upon them to demand cash advance which, though it rendered them in one way 'bonded' to the system, also enabled them to build up considerable financial assets and an independence unknown to the other workers.

To sum up, the case studies in this volume reveal a wide variety of forms of resistance to bondage – some successful, some less so – in the IOW. Taken together, they add an important dimension to what we know about slave systems and slavery in the IOW and provide a further comparative perspective on studies of slavery globally.

Notes

1 Gwyn Campbell, 'Unfree labour, slavery and protest in Imperial Madagascar' in this volume.
2 Edward A. Alpers, Gwyn Campbell and Michael Salman (eds), *Slavery, Forced Labour and Resistance in Indian Ocean Africa and Asia* (London: Routledge, 2005); Gwyn Campbell (ed.), *The Structure of Slavery in Indian Ocean Africa and Asia* (London: Frank Cass, 2004).
3 G. Roger Knight, 'Sugar and servility: themes of forced labour, resistance and accommodation in mid-nineteenth century Java'; Francesca Declich, 'Unfree labour, forced labour and resistance among the Zigula of the Lower Juba' – both in this volume.
4 Isabelle Denis, 'Forced labour and the 1856 revolt on Mayotta' in this volume.
5 Nigel Worden, 'Revolt in Cape Colony slave society' in this volume.
6 Knight, 'Sugar and servility'.
7 Shigeru Sato, 'Forced labourers and their resistance in Java under Japanese Military Rule, 1942–45' in this volume.
8 Campbell, 'Unfree labour'; Eric Jennings, 'Forced labour in Madagascar under Vichy, 1940–42: autarky, forced labour and resistance on the 'Red Island' – both in this volume.
9 Campbell, 'Unfree labour'.
10 Robert Castle, Jim Hagan and Andrew Wells, '"Unfree" labour on the cattle stations of Northern Australia, the tea gardens of Assam, and the rubber plantations of Indo-China, 1920–50' in this volume
11 Knight, 'Sugar and servility'.
12 Gwyn Campbell, *Brigandry and Revolt in Pre-Colonial Africa: Imperial Madagascar, 1750–1900* (in preparation).
13 Castle, Hagan and Wells, '"Unfree" labour'.
14 Castle, Hagan and Wells, '"Unfree" labour'; Gwyn Campbell, Suzanne Miers and Joseph C. Miller (eds), *Women and Slavery* (Athens, OH: Ohio University Press, 2007, forthcoming).
15 Castle, Hagan and Wells, '"Unfree" labour'.
16 Campbell, 'Unfree labour'.
17 Ibid.
18 Worden, 'Revolt'.
19 Jennings, 'Forced labour'.
20 Campbell, 'Unfree labour'.
21 Castle, Hagan and Wells, '"Unfree" labour'.

2 Revolt in Cape Colony slave society

Nigel Worden

Introduction

Major slave revolts, such as those led by Spartacus or Nat Turner or the successful uprising of eighteenth-century Haitian slaves have a prominent place in our thinking about slave resistance. But their very rarity in world history explains the attention given to them. Much more typical were slave societies in which massive and unified slave revolt did not occur, but instead small-scale, day-to-day resistance of the unfree against their owners was endemic. And if more concerted revolt did break out it was usually on a smaller scale and less successful than these well-known examples.

The Cape was one such society. It lacked a plantation economy characteristic of many European colonies in the Americas, but much of its rural and urban economy was dependent on slave labour. Located at the dividing point between the Atlantic and Indian Ocean worlds, it imported between 1658 and 1807 over 60,000 slaves from Asia, Madagascar and eastern Africa which together with locally born slaves and unfree indigenous Khoi and San labourers at least equalled, and sometimes outnumbered, European settlers and officials throughout the eighteenth and early decades of the nineteenth century.[1]

Forms of resistance

The Cape colony lacked large-scale slave rebellions, but their very absence has been cause of much debate. To writers before the 1970s this was explained by the assumption that Cape slavery was peculiarly benign, and that slaves therefore had no cause to rise up against their protecting owners.[2] But the 'first generation' of revisionist historians of the late 1970s and 1980s convincingly destroyed this view of the well-treated Cape slave.[3] The dilemma was still to explain the absence of revolt.

The model for such a task came from the vibrant work of slave historians of the Atlantic World. Absence of revolt was explained by structural forces. Drawing especially on the ideas of Eugene Genovese and Michael Craton, Cape revisionist historians argued that the colony lacked the features which tended to produce massive revolt in the Americas, notably absentee owners, economic distress, slaveholding units of several hundred people, divisions within the master class and the heavy outnumbering of colonists and settlers by slaves. None of these conditions existed in the small-scale slaveholdings of the households and farmsteads of the Cape.[4] Other factors identified by the Atlantic historians did apply to the Cape. Foreign-born slaves predominated over locally born creoles throughout the eighteenth century, and the geography of the colony enabled flight into the interior away from settler control. But both of these factors encouraged escape and flight rather than revolt.

Robert Ross' pioneering study of Cape slave resistance documented the prevalence of escape, and later historians confirmed his analysis.[5] As early as the year of the first slave imports in 1658, the colonists returned half of their slaves to the Company on the grounds that 'it had become quite evident that they were naturally inclined to run away in spite of being well treated'.[6] Out of the hundreds of examples of slave desertion that litter the pages of the archival records, some broad features are evident. Slaves usually ran away individually or in small groups, and more frequently in summer when weather conditions favoured life in the open and the demands of harvest time made work routines more onerous than usual. There were favoured routes of escape: from Cape Town up into Table Mountain and then across the Cape Flats that joined the early settlement to the African interior. Most deserters were male, only partly because of the gendered imbalance in the slave population as a whole. The majority were also foreign-born, with memories of a life of freedom.

Some returned after short periods on the run, but others were determined never to do so.[7] Some were re-captured, but many were not. Groups of *drosters* (escapees) lived on Table Mountain, where they exchanged wood for food with urban slaves; their fires alarmed the inhabitants of the town below. A maroon community of about 100 slaves lived at Cape Hangklip, a promontory at the mouth of False Bay within sight of Table Mountain, from at least the 1720s into the nineteenth century. They survived by raiding nearby farms and wagons passing over the mountains from the interior as well as by fishing in the bay. We know that some slaves escaped from the colony altogether: to the Orange River some 600 kilometres north of Cape Town where together with the local Khoi, San and other European deserters from the colony they formed the basis of the 'Bastaard' and Oorlam communities of the late eighteenth and nineteenth centuries, east to the Xhosa and possibly further afield.[8] A few managed to stow away on passing ships.[9] And there were many *drosters* whose fates will never be known.

A recently discovered list of slave *drosters* from Cape Town and its immediate vicinity for the period January 1806 to June 1809 confirms a picture of the prevalence of slave desertion.[10] In this period of three and a half years, a total of 754 slaves were reported missing, some eight per cent of the slave population of the town. Ninety per cent were male: since by this stage the proportion of males to females in the slave population of the town was 2:1, these figures reveal a much higher propensity for men to escape than for women.[11] Eighty-three per cent of the *drosters* were foreign-born, even though by this stage the majority of urban slaves were locally born. Many (280 or 37 per cent) came from Mozambique and were young males brought to the colony in the preceding decade.[12] Only 159 (21 per cent) returned or were recaptured. Most escaped for brief periods (sometimes only a day or two), and only exceptionally were *drosters* absent for more than a month. It seems that most slaves escaped entirely, while a few took brief periods of unauthorized absence, most often in the summer months.

Other forms of overt resistance sometimes accompanied desertion. Attacks on property, especially firing crops just before the harvest, or on owners was not unusual and usually preceded flight. Such periodic attacks rocked the colony. In 1760 a group of slaves murdered their Cape Town owners and fled to the mountain.[13] In 1803 the village of Stellenbosch was badly gutted by fire started by a group of slaves who planned to seize booty and then escape.[14]

Escape, whether permanently or in the short term, was usually an individual response and one which led to an abandonment of the colony and of the other slaves in it. Rebellion was collective and sought the overturn of slavery in the colony. The prevalence of desertion, and the absence of rebellion, at the Cape has been explained by the 'atomization' of the Cape slave population.[15] This was true geographically – slaves were scattered over a wide area, in small units, often with only a handful of other slaves working alongside them. But Ross and I have also argued that in the seventeenth and eighteenth centuries, the very diverse geographical origins of slaves also inhibited the development of a unified 'slave' cultural identity. Slaves from different regions of South Asia, Southeast Asia, Madagascar, Mozambique and elsewhere worked alongside each other, speaking diverse and mutually unintelligible languages, possessing widely differing beliefs, traditions and memories. Although slaves in the Atlantic colonies also came from widely differing societies and cultures within Africa, the regions of high incidence of revolt tended to be ones where there was a degree of ethnic or cultural unity among the slave rebels.[16]

This is not of course to argue that Cape slaves lacked a 'culture'. Rather it is to stress that the emergence of a distinctive Cape slave identity was less easy than in societies where slaves came from a more homogeneous source of origin, and that this inhibited collective forms of resistance. And this argument is perhaps supported by the fact that as creolization took place in the early nineteenth century when a higher proportion of Cape slaves were locally born, spoke the same language (creolized Afrikaans) and shared the same life-long experiences of servitude in the colony, collective revolt did take place.[17]

Slave revolt

There were two occasions when Cape slaves rebelled against their owners and demanded freedom and rights within the colony, rather than seeking to escape from it: in Genovese's terms these were thus 'revolutions' rather than 'rebellions'.[18] As both were small scale and neither succeeded,[19] they have not entered the Big League of global slave revolts. However, their occurrence points to important shifts in the character of Cape slave resistance in the early nineteenth century.

The first revolt took place in 1808.[20] Two slaves, Louis van Mauritius and Abraham van der Caap, were discussing the recent ending of the slave trade with two Irish ex-employees of the East India Company who had recently arrived in the town. The Irishmen declared that 'there were no slaves in their country and that consequently there ought to be none here'.[21] Determined to fight for freedom for all slaves, they persuaded some 320 male slaves from the Koeberg farming region in the Cape Town hinterland to march on the town and demand emancipation. As the march proceeded farms were looted, owners taken captive and one settler woman raped. At Salt River, as they approached the town, they were defeated by the militia. Louis, Abraham and three other slave ringleaders (including the rapist) were executed.

There are several notable features of this episode. First, Louis was no ordinary slave. Imported from Mauritius, he was part of the new slaving networks established by the British in the south-west Indian Ocean and this in itself made him both a relative newcomer from an unusual background (in a sample database of slaves by place of origin dating from 1816, only nine from a total of 5,703 came from Mauritius).[22] Moreover he worked on his own accord as a tailor in Cape Town and there is evidence that he lived apart from his owner with a 'wife' (formal marriage for slaves was illegal). He was thus likely to have been particularly attracted by the prospect of a legal freedom from which he would be well able to benefit. The same could not have been said for many of the farm slaves who followed him and for whom notions of freedom would be at best hazy. But the sight of Louis who dressed himself as a 'Spanish captain' in 'a blue jacket with red collar and cuffs, a large and small sword, two gold and two silver epaulets and some ostrich feathers' was sufficient to persuade them that here was a man to be taken note of as 'the acknowledged head of the rebellion'.[23]

However, it was not only Louis the tailor's symbolic dress sense that attracted their attention. The timing of his clarion call was not coincidental. The ending of the slave trade in January 1808 had created a great deal of anxiety among slave-owners, and the activities of reformists (not yet abolitionists) in Britain and the Caribbean were known at the Cape. The very existence of the list of slaves who had escaped between 1806 and 1809 is testimony to the concern of the government about the effect of abolitionist ideas on the slave population.[24] Such anxiety was readily perceived by the slaves. New notions of freedom were emerging in ways which had never been heard before.[25] Thus Louis determined that he should demand from the Governor the 'liberty of the slaves of this colony, and in case of a refusal make themselves masters of the Magazines, to storm and force the Prison, release the prisoners, and fight for the liberty of the slaves'.[26] He informed the workers on the farms he visited that 'all Christians should be bound and brought to Cape Town, where they would be sent overseas, and the land would belong to the slaves'.[27] As Ross has pointed out, the target of their attack was property – 34 farms were looted, especially for guns, clothing, horses and ammunition – rather than the owners themselves.[28] Of particular significance is that in the looting of farmsteads papers and documents, the symbols of the authority of purchase deeds, auctions and laws that slaves were denied access to because of their inability to read, were 'tor[n] to pieces'.[29] Some 30 farmers were captured, usually with violence, but no-one was killed and in some cases women and children were left alone. One slave raped a farmer's wife, but not the women on his owner's farm.[30] It was freedom and property that the workers wanted, not the lives of their masters, although Abraham's assertion that after victory, 'the slave girls in their turn could say *sy* [a disrespectful expression in the Dutch language] to their mistresses' indicates that they looked forward to a reversal of social roles.[31]

Karen Harris has argued that the uprising cannot be described as a rebellion, let alone a revolution, on the grounds that it was not a consciously pre-planned and organized event but rather spontaneous and haphazard.[32] There was little sign of collective slave solidarity; some slaves protected their owners and ran away from the rebels while others claimed at their trial that they had only acted out of fear. On the grounds that they had been passive participants, 244 of the marchers were returned to their owners 'with a serious warning'.[33] Harris sees the events of 1808 as another indicator of the incapacity of Cape slaves to organize collective resistance.[34] Certainly the limited effectiveness of the uprising is clear. But revolts are rarely smooth and never command total loyalty. It is true that the revolutionary character of the uprising may be questioned. Although the demand for emancipation and banishment of all 'Christians' was certainly radical, Louis made his followers believe that his actions were ordained by the Fiscal (the public prosecutor) and the Governor themselves, and many slaves thought that these 'great men' had summoned them to assemble with their captured masters in Cape Town.[35] They were, as usual, merely obeying instructions, albeit from a different source. Even if this may have been true of many of the rebels, it was not so for their more realistic leaders, one of whom declared that they would 'hoist the bloody flag and fight themselves free'.[36] There is no doubt that the actions, goals and ideological impetus of the Tygerberg march was a significant rebellious challenge to Cape slaveholding society and one which the authorities were unlikely to forget.

The second uprising took place in 1825 on a remote farm named ironically, and with a notable lack of charm, Hou-den-Bek ('Shut Your Mouth') in the Bokkeveld, a barren and mountainous region about 250 kilometres from Cape Town.[37] A number of slave and Khoi labourers, led by the slave Galant van de Caap, killed the farmer and some of his family, and threatened to take over other farms in the region. They were captured and subsequently executed, but their actions severely alarmed the slave-owners of the colony.

Although this episode was on a much smaller scale than the 1808 uprising – the 13 rebels were captured before they could leave Hou-den-Bek – the two events were not unconnected. As the Fiscal claimed at the subsequent trial, 'the pernicious poison of strife and discontent infused into the minds of the slaves' in 1808 had not been quelled, 'still however the fire of discontent at the general hope of a general freedom appears to have been smouldering under the ashes, so that the smallest blast of wind is but necessary to make the flame burst out again more violently than ever'.[38] For, 'it was not the ill treatment which Galant alleges to have suffered that brought him to the step, as he calls it, of fighting himself free; no, it was his disappointed hopes of freedom that induced him to it.'[39]

Again the timing of the revolt was significant. For in 1825, the British government was implementing 'reforms' in its slave colonies. In 1816, farmers had been forced to register their slaves, in order to prevent their illegal importation and sale. In 1823, further regulations were passed which owners viewed as an onslaught on their rights over the slaves. These included restrictions on amount of punishment, minimum requirements for food and clothing, limitations on hours of work and a ban on the sale of young slave children without their mothers.[40] Slaves were now entitled to report to the authorities if their owners failed to comply with such measures, and indeed Galant had complained to the Worcester magistrate that his master had unfairly and excessively punished him.

Although Galant's complaint was dismissed and he received only further punishment for his pains, this assertion of his new-found rights may explain the virulence of his owner's reactions to government reforms. In the remote Bokkeveld it was feared that the new British colonial government planned complete emancipation. As Galant reported at his trial, anger at such audacity led his owner's wife to fulminate that it was

> said in the Newspapers that the slaves must be free, but if the Farmers would not allow it then it would not take place, to which I did not say anything . . . Some time after, another Newspaper came, when my wife [the Khoi house servant Betje] told me that her Mistress had said that the first Englishman who came to make the slaves free should be shot, as well as the slaves . . . [41]

Galant stated that he later overheard his owner saying to another farmer that 'he must keep himself armed in order to shoot the first Commissioner or Englishman who should come to the Country to make the Slaves free together with the Slaves all in one heap'.[42]

It is likely that Galant emphasized such episodes at his trial in order better to justify his subsequent actions as those of pre-emptive self-defence. There is plenty of evidence to suggest that he was also deeply aggrieved at punishments and slights he had suffered at the hands of his master, with whom he been brought up as a child on the farm. Nonetheless, it is clear that his owners did fear the changes taking place in the Cape's slave system at the time, and rumours spread by them would certainly have been heard by their slaves. The significance of the written word is again apparent. In 1825, the only newspaper in the Colony, *The South African Commercial Advertiser*, took a broadly pro-abolitionist line under its editor John Fairbairn and it was not until 1830 that *De Zuid-Afrikaan* newspaper was founded to counteract such ideologies.[43] Clearly the *Advertiser*'s line was not only unappreciated by many farmers, but its (far from radical) ameliorative tone was greatly exaggerated by them – and hence by their slaves. Galant had his own motives for revenge but he was also spurred by the belief that he was acting in the spirit of ideas supported by the authorities: a rebel with charisma, but not a revolutionary.

Patricia van der Spuy has highlighted the gendered feature of the Bokkeveld revolt.[44] All of the participants were male, with the exception of one female slave, Pamela van de Kaap, and her role was entirely passive. As was the case in 1808, not only was this a revolt of the unfree, it was also a revolt of unfree men. Van der Spuy argues that Galant's owner's control over both his wife (whom he used as a sexual partner) and his son (whom he punished) denied Galant not only his personal dignity but also his masculinity. Such an argument is supported by Pamela Scully's demonstration of the assertiveness of ex-slave men after emancipation and their denial of female sexual and economic independence.[45] It would seem that revolt, as with desertion, was a highly gendered process.

Revolts of the unfree

There was another feature of the 1808 and 1825 revolts which points to a much neglected factor in the historiography of the early Cape Colony. Although overwhelmingly carried out by slaves, neither was a protest by slaves alone. The marchers of 1808 were joined by several Khoi, although we lack precise figures.[46] Dirk Jager, 'though a Hottentot and a free man'[47] readily joined the rebels as did Arie Abel a Khoi labourer. In 1825 the court prosecutor dismissed Galant's claim that he and his followers were fighting for a freedom that was rightfully theirs on the grounds that there were 'a number of Hottentots among them who although they lived in the Service and under the control of the Christian Inhabitants, had nothing to do with the idea of a release from a state of Slavery, which did not exist ... [for them]'.[48] A 'free European', Petrus Josephus de Campher, who was working at Hou-den-Bek during the harvest, also encouraged Galant, although he was absent when the revolt broke out.

This points to a crucial factor in Cape slave society. Slaves were not the only unfree labourers in the colony, and to view them in isolation is misleading.[49] The circumstances under which Khoi labourers worked on settler farms in practice differed little from that of slaves.[50] Also, although the Khoi were legally free, by the mid-late eighteenth century Cape courts were blurring the distinction between free and slave in important respects: seizure of Khoi livestock was condoned and Khoi testimony was disregarded unless backed by a settler.[51] Increasingly as Khoi lost their stock as well as their land, a common culture of a slave and Khoi proletarianized rural workforce emerged (marked, for instance, by the use of creole Dutch influenced by Khoi and slave syntactic structures and vocabulary which was to become known as Afrikaans.)[52]

The system of indenture (*inboekstelsel*) formalized clientage in ways which approximated much more closely to coerced labour.[53] Often loosely (and euphemistically) referred to as 'apprenticeship', *inboekstelsel* contained no provision for training and was direct labour indenture. There is evidence that *inboekseling* rights were bought and sold and settler commando raids by the late eighteenth century were taking children 'abandoned' by their parents (often orphaned by commando attacks) and indenturing them under the *inboekstelsel* system, a practice which differed only in name from slave raiding.[54] There was little likelihood that such captives would ever regain any independence, even after the formal ending of their indenture.

And open rebellion followed. Between 1799 and 1803, hundreds of Khoi and San farm workers abandoned their employers and made joint cause with the Xhosa who were resisting colonial encroachment on their land in the eastern Graaff-Reinet district of the colony.[55] Forming themselves into bands with a command structure that closely resembled those of their ancestors, they inflicted severe blows on settler farms as far west as the Swellendam district in the middle of the colony. The British, who had taken over the Cape in 1795, were alarmed, not least by the rocketing price of meat in Cape Town that resulted from the disruption of the eastern districts. Military forces sent from Cape Town led to the rebellion's defeat.

The 1808 uprising was thus part of a broader and longer-standing pattern of revolt by the unfree. In the atmosphere of settler fear that came in its wake, the Caledon Code of 1809 'institutional[ized] the servile status of the colonial Khoi and San, while extending the rule of law at the Cape.'[56] It stipulated that every 'Hottentot' should henceforth have a specific place of abode which in the context of the completed process of settler land expropriation effectively meant as a farm worker.[57] Those found outside farms without a pass signed by an employer were liable to arrest on a charge of vagrancy and could be compelled to enter into a labour contract. The Caledon Code has been seen as the height of colonial regulated labour coercion over the Khoi and San, effectively reducing them to 'aliens in their own land'.

The focus of abolitionist work in the Cape Colony was consequently aimed as much, or more, at the indentured and coerced Khoi as it was at the slaves.[58] Considerable impetus was given by the fear of united rebellion by the rural proletariat of Khoi and slaves which the Bokkeveld uprising of 1825 evoked. Three years later, the colonial government passed Ordinance 50 which removed the restrictions of the Caledon Code, a move which favoured the mobility of labour to the expanding new pastoral farms of the eastern Cape. But it also defused some of the resentment that was brewing among Khoi workers on the farmers.

However, the fear, and the reality, of rural labour unrest was rekindled after emancipation. Slave and Khoi expectations in the decades after the 1830s were severely prescribed by the lack of access to land and capital. The result was far from 'freedom'; continued proletarianization as low-paid farm workers was the fate of most ex-slaves and Khoi. Soon after, emancipation legislation was introduced which drew on the previous traditions of Khoi and San labour control to regulate all farm workers. The Master and Servant Ordinance of 1841 stipulated the need for labour contracts but was heavily weighed in the favour of employers. 'Misconduct' by servants, defined as including negligent work, insolence, immorality and absence, was made a criminal offence, punishable by fines or withholding of wages. Special magistrates, initially appointed to administer the apprenticeship regulations in the mid-1830s, were retained to deal with the stream of cases that flooded the local courts, the majority brought by farmers against 'disobedient' workers.[59]

The situation in the eastern Cape differed somewhat, largely because some slaves and Khoi labourers had obtained or retained access to land for their own use.[60] In the 1830s, many Khoi and slave workers left the settler farms. Some formed armed gangs and wreaked revenge by plunder, but others established themselves in peasant communities either on lands on the margins of settler farms or in areas abandoned by Dutch farmers who had trekked out of the colony. The largest peasant community was established at the Kat River Settlement, granted by the government in 1828 on land confiscated from Xhosa farmers in the aftermath of fierce conflict. Such communities were bitterly resented by settler farmers, who in the 1840s increasingly found support from a state which was more interested in backing commercial wool farming by settlers than peasant production. What has been described as a 'frontal attack' on peasant cultivators took place with livestock impoundment, retroactive rate levies, refusal of access to roads and markets and finally a Squatting Bill which forbade occupation of unoccupied crown land.[61]

The result was a major rebellion in 1850–53 led by, but not confined to, the Kat River Settlement, in which Khoi and ex-slave rebels made common cause with the Xhosa and attacked the colonists. Although it was feared that the rebellion might spread, the western Cape remained unaffected: here there was no recent tradition of independent cultivation to defend. But in the eastern Cape the rebellion marked a final onslaught on independent peasant farmers, this time by British troops. The Kat River rebels were dispossessed, and the Squatting Ordinance became law. The rebellion in the eastern Cape severely unnerved colonists and the government in the arable districts of the western Cape, in a situation which one historian has described as the 'Great Fear' of the Cape countryside.[62] Rumours began in 1851, when the eastern Cape revolt was underway, that the Khoi and ex-slaves (now described as 'coloured') of the western Cape mission stations and farms were planning to rise up against the farmers. The settlers had reason enough for concern, given the example of the eastern Cape rebels and the frustrated expectations of emancipation, the continued poverty and the oppressive controls of the 1841 Masters and Servants Act. In the words of the governor, Sir Harry Smith, there was 'almost general dissatisfaction of the coloured classes within the colony'.[63] Farmers formed commandos for self-defence and talked of pre-emptive strikes against supposed centres of sedition, notably the mission stations whose inhabitants they had long resented.

The 'great fear' came to nothing, but there is no doubt that the rumours of revolt were not completely unfounded. In this atmosphere many abolitionists who had campaigned for Khoi freedom in 1828 and supported slave emancipation in the 1830s were disillusioned and there were few colonists who backed the rights of ex-slaves to independence.[64] When in 1853 the Cape Colony acquired self-government, a combination of squatting legislation and a new Masters and Servants Act (1856) increased controls over labour and made independent production virtually impossible. The resentment and resistance of the freed slave and Khoi labourers at the Cape led, as in Jamaica after the Morant Bay revolt of 1865, to a marked increase in racial tensions in the post-emancipation era.[65]

Notes

1 For general studies of Cape slavery and unfree labour see especially, R. Ross, *Cape of Torments: Slavery and Resistance in South Africa* (London: Routledge, 1983); N. Worden, *Slavery in Dutch South Africa* (Cambridge: Cambridge University Press, 1985); R. Elphick and H. Giliomee (eds), *The Shaping of South African Society, 1652–1840*, 2nd edn. (Cape Town: Maskew Miller Longman, 1989); R. Shell, *Children of Bondage: a Social History of the Slave Society at the Cape of Good Hope, 1652–1838* (Johannesburg: Witwatersrand University Press, 1994); T. Keegan, *Colonial South Africa and the Origins of the Racial Order* (Cape Town: David Philip, 1996).

2 The most prominent example of this apologist approach is V. de Kock, *Those in Bondage: An Account of the Life of the Slave at the Cape in the Days of the Dutch East India Company* (Port Washington: Kennikat Press, 1950). Denying the need for rebellion, de Kock nonetheless explains the high incidence of escape: 'many of the slaves had so little taste for work that they had scarcely arrived at the Cape when they began to desert, in the vague hope of either regaining the land of their birth or leading the carefree life of the natives, maintaining themselves in the mountains and committing atrocious crimes and depredations' – de Kock, *Those in Bondage*, p. 71. Such racist views swiftly percolated into local school textbooks of the apartheid era and are consequently still prevalent among some South Africans today.

3 A description used by later writers to refer to the works of Ross and Worden cited above, as well as the pioneering articles by L. Greenstein, 'Slave and citizen: the South African case', *Race* 15 (1973), pp. 25–46 and J. Armstrong, 'The slaves, 1652–1795' in R. Elphick and H. Giliomee (eds), *The Shaping of South African Society, 1652–1820* 1st edn. (Cape Town: Maskew Miller Longman, 1979).

4 This list of conditions favouring slave revolt comes from E. Genovese, *From Rebellion to Revolution: Afro-American Slave Revolts in The Making of the New World* (New York: Vintage Books, 1979), pp. 11–12. See also M. Craton, *Testing the Chains: Resistance to Slavery in the British West Indies* (Ithaca: Cornell University Press, 1982).

5 Ross, *Cape of Torments*; Worden, *Slavery*, ch. 9. For the prevalence of escape in slave societies throughout the Indian Ocean region, see N. Alpers, 'Flight to freedom: escape from slavery among bonded Africans in the Indian Ocean world, *c*.1750–1962', Workshop on Slave Systems in Asia and the Indian Ocean, CERINS, Université d'Avignon, May 2000.

6 H. B. Thom (ed.), *Daghregister van Van Riebeeck* (Cape Town: Balkema, 1952), II, p. 371.

7 This is the distinction which Alpers in 'Flight to Freedom' refers to as 'petit' and 'grand' maronnage. The difference was not always apparent and was often circumstantial. Inability to obtain food was often a reason why those who intended to be 'grands' marroons ended up as 'petits'.

8 N. Penn 'The Northern Cape Frontier Zone, 1700– *c*.1815', PhD, University of Cape Town, 1995; N. Penn, 'The Orange River Frontier Zone, *c*.1700[–]1805' in A. Smith (ed.), *Einiqualand: Studies of the Orange River Frontier* (Cape Town: University of Cape Town Press, 1995) especially pp. 34–8.

9 For example, Cape (Roeland Street) Archives, Crimineele regtsrollen, 18 February 1751, case of Jan van de Kaap, CJ 33, 31–2 and Crimineele regtsrollen, 20 April 1752, case of Jacob van de Kaap, CJ 34, 28–30. Both escaped to Holland but were recaptured when they made a return visit to the Cape as enlisted crewmen of the VOC.

10 Cape Archives, Roeland Street (CA), A 50 (2), 23: Register van absente slaven. I am grateful to Robert Ross for drawing my attention to this valuable document.

11 Figures for 1806 calculated in A. Bank, *The Decline of Urban Slavery at the Cape, 1806 to 1834*, Centre for African Studies, University of Cape Town, Communications No. 22 (1991), p. 233.

12 On the regions of origin and the increase in south-east African slave imports in the late eighteenth and early nineteenth centuries, see N. Worden, 'The Indian Ocean origins of Cape Colony slaves: a preliminary report', Workshop on Slave Systems in Asia and the Indian Ocean, CERINS, Université d'Avignon, May 2000 and 'Indian Ocean Slavery and its Demise in the Cape Colony', in Gwyn Campbell (ed.), *Abolition and Its Aftermath in Indian Ocean Africa and Asia* (London: Routledge, 2005), pp. 29–49; M. Reidy, 'The admission of slaves and "prize slaves" into the Cape Colony, 1797–1818', MA thesis, University of Cape Town, 1997; R. Ross, 'The last years of the slave trade to the Cape Colony', *Slavery and Abolition* 9.3 (1988), pp. 209–19.

13 M. Cairns, 'The Smuts family murders – 14.4.1760', *CABO* 2 (1980), pp. 13–16.

14 M. Lichtenstein, *Travels in Southern Africa in the Years 1803–1806* (Cape Town: Van Riebeeck Society: 1930), p. 128.

15 Ross, *Cape of Torments*, especially pp. 117–18; Worden, *Slavery*, p. 120.

16 For example, J. J. Reis, *Slave Rebellion in Brazil: The Muslim Uprising of 1835 in Bahia* (Baltimore: Johns Hopkins University Press, 1993), pp. 139–41.

17 On creolization see especially A. M. Rugarli, 'Slavery at the Cape Colony: from

acquisition to the process of creolization, *c*.1790–1830', Tesi di Laurea, Facolta' di Scienze Politiche, Universita' degli Studi di Milano, 1997–98, ch. 2.

18 Genovese, *From Rebellion to Revolution.*

19 The best account of the two revolts is given in Ross, *Cape of Torments*, ch. 8, somewhat ironically entitled 'The impossibility of rebellion'.

20 On this revolt see Karen Harris, 'The slave 'rebellion' of 1808', *Kleio* (Pretoria), 20 (1988), pp. 54–65 and D. Joubert, 'Die slawe opstand van 1808 in die Koe-Tygerberg en Swartland distrikte', MA thesis, University of South Africa, 1946. The court records are in CA, CJ 514–16 and the sentence is translated in G. Theal, *Records of Cape Colony*, (London: Clowes Printers for the Government of the Cape Colony, 1900) VI, pp. 408–41.

21 Theal, *Records*, VI, p. 411.

22 Worden, 'Indian Ocean slavery in the Cape Colony', Table 2.

23 Theal, *Records*, VI, pp. 411 and 420.

24 CA, A50(2), 23, analysed above.

25 Harris, 'Slave 'rebellion'' denies that there is evidence for this, but Louis's own words and actions are a clear demonstration of the spreading of such news.

26 Theal, *Records*, VI, p. 412.

27 Ross, *Cape of Torments*, p. 100.

28 Ibid. p. 102.

29 Theal, *Records*, VI, p. 417.

30 Ibid. pp. 415, 422.

31 *Sy* is a misprint in Theal's printed version of the trial record. The word is *jij*, a term indicating familiarity or superiority, and used in Dutch by parents speaking to children or owners to their slaves – see Theal, *Records*, VI, p. 420.

32 Harris, 'Slave 'rebellion'' especially pp. 63–4.

33 Theal, *Records*, VI, p. 418.

34 Harris, 'Slave 'rebellion'', especially pp. 64–5.

35 Theal, *Records*, VI, pp. 414–16, 433.

36 Ibid. p. 420.

37 The 'Galant revolt' forms the basis of Andre Brink's evocative novel *Hou-den-Bek* (Cape Town: Tafelberg, 1982) translated as *Chain of Voices* (London: Fontana, 1982). See also P. G. Warnich, 'Die toepassing en invloed van slawewetgewing in die landdrosdistrik Tulbagh/Worcester, 1816–1830', MA thesis, University of Stellenbosch, 1988, chs. 4–5. The archival documentation is found in CA,CJ 633 and CJ 819 and is printed in Theal, *Records of Cape Colony* (London: Clowes Printers for the Government of the Cape Colony, 1904) XX, pp. 188–341.

38 Theal, *Records* XX, pp. 314–15.

39 Theal, *Records* XX, p. 318.

40 Warnich, 'Die toepassing', chs. 2–3.

41 Theal, *Records* XX, p. 209.

42 Theal, *Records* XX, p. 210.

43 On the impact of the *Commercial Advertiser* see Kirsten McKenzie, 'The *South African Commercial Advertiser* and the making of middle class identity in early nineteenth century Cape Town', MA thesis, University of Cape Town, 1993.

44 P. van der Spuy, 'A collection of discrete essays with the common theme of gender and slavery at the Cape of Good Hope, with a focus on the 1820s', MA thesis, University of Cape Town, 1993, paper 5; 'Making himself master: Galant's rebellion revisited', *South African Historical Journal* 34 (1996), pp. 1–28.

45 Pamela Scully, *Liberating the family?: Gender and British Slave Emancipation in the Rural Western Cape, 1823–1853* (Cape Town: David Philip, 1997).

46 The names of only 98 out of some 300 participants are known from the court records. Of these, two were Khoi labourers, Theal, *Records*, VI, pp. 408–9.

47 Theal, *Records*, VI, p. 428.

48 Theal, *Records*, XX, p. 192.

49 Khoi and San labour was particularly important on the settler farms of the northern and eastern Cape where slaves were less affordable, less skilled in pastoral work and less easy to prevent from escaping into the interior. But even on the wine and arable farms of the Stellenbosch district close to Cape Town, well over half of the farmers in 1806 employed Khoi workers, Worden, *Slavery in Dutch South Africa*, p. 35.

50 Russell Viljoen, 'Khoi and San labour relations in the Overburg districts during the latter half of the eighteenth century, *c.*1755–1795', MA thesis, University of the Western Cape, 1993, Susan Newton-King, *Masters and Servants on the Cape Eastern Frontier, 1760–1803* (Cambridge: Cambridge University Press, 1999); C. Malherbe, 'Diversification and mobility of Khoikhoi labour in the eastern districts of Cape Colony prior to the labour law of 1 November 1809', MA thesis, University of Cape Town, 1978.

51 Robert Ross, 'The changing legal position of the Khoi and San in the Cape Colony, 1652–1795' in Robert Ross, *Beyond the Pale: Essays in the History of Colonial South Africa* (Johannesburg: Witwatersrand University Press, 1993), pp. 166–80.

52 Hans den Besten, 'From Khoekhoe foreignertalk via Hottentot Dutch to Afrikaans: the creation of a novel grammar', in M. Pütz and R. Dirven (eds) *Wheel Within Wheels* (Frankfurt: Peter Lang, 1989), pp. 207–54.

53 Candy Malherbe, 'Indentured and unfree labour in South Africa: towards an understanding', *South African Historical Journal* 24 (1991), p. 15; Hermann Giliomee, 'Processes in the development of the Southern African frontier', in Howard Lamar and Leonard Thompson (eds), *The Frontier in History: North America and Southern Africa Compared* (New Haven: Yale University Press, 1981), p. 85.

54 Fred Morton, 'Slavery in South Africa', in Elizabeth Eldredge and Fred Morton (eds), *Slavery in South Africa: Captive Labour on the Dutch Frontier* (Boulder: Westview Press and Pietermaritzburg: University of Natal Press, 1994), pp. 258–9. The editors of this collection claim that all forms of labour incorporation in this period were equivalent to African practices of domestic slavery, but their argument has not found general acceptance; see for instance, Keegan, *Colonial South Africa*, p. 297.

55 Susan Newton-King and Candy Malherbe, 'The Khoikhoi Rebellion in the Eastern Cape (1799–1803)', Centre for African Studies, University of Cape Town, Communications No. 5 (1981).

56 Keegan, *Colonial South Africa*, p. 35.

57 Contrary to some interpretations of the code, both by contemporaries and by modern historians, Khoi landholding was not legally forbidden.

58 For the nature of Cape abolitionism and emancipation, see Worden, 'The slave system of the Cape Colony'.

59 Scully, *Liberating the family?*, p. 163; N. Worden, 'Adjusting to emancipation: freed slaves and farmers in the mid nineteenth century south-western Cape', in Wilmot James and Mary Simons (eds), *The Angry Divide: Social and Economic History of the Western Cape* (Cape Town: David Philip, 1989), pp. 37–8.

60 John Mason, 'Fortunate slaves and artful masters', in Eldredge and Morton (eds), *Slavery in South Africa*, pp. 67–91.

61 Clifton Crais, 'Slavery and emancipation in the eastern Cape', in Nigel Worden and Clifton Crais (eds), *Breaking the Chains: Slavery and its Legacy in the Nineteenth-Century Cape Colony* (Johannesburg: Witwatersrand University Press, 1994), pp. 271–87.

62 Edna Bradlow, '"The Great Fear" at the Cape of Good Hope, 1851–2', *International Journal of African Historical Studies* 22.2 (1989), pp. 401–22.

63 Cited in Ibid. p. 406.
64 The disillusionment of the humanitarian abolitionists and the growth of racist discourse in the mid-nineteenth century was widespread in the Britain and its colonies. For the Cape, see Andrew Bank, 'Liberals and their enemies: racial ideology at the Cape of Good Hope, 1820 to 1850', PhD thesis, Cambridge University, 1995.
65 G. Heuman, *'The Killing Time': The Morant Bay Rebellion in Jamaica* (London: Macmillan, 1994); Douglas Lorimer, *Colour, Class and the Victorians: English Attitudes to the Negro in the Mid-nineteenth Century* (Leicester: Leicester University Press, 1978), pp. 178–200.

3 Unfree labour, forced labour and resistance among the Zigula of the Lower Juba

*Francesca Declich**

Introduction

Interpreting resistance to forced labour during the colonial period is a complex issue, especially in countries where several forms of slavery were common before colonialism and where colonial policies tended to implement emancipation decrees gradually rather than put abolition into immediate effect.

This chapter deals with episodes of resistance to forced labour in agricultural concessions held by Italian farmers in the Lower Juba River region of southern Somalia until 1941 and during the Second World War when the colony came under the direction of the British Military Administration (BMA). The region, then known as Oltregiuba to the Italians, as ex-Jubaland to the British and as Gosha to the Somalis, had been transferred from the British protectorate to the Italian colonial government in 1925. During the colonial period, the Italian press sometimes denied the existence of forced labour in Somalia,[1] but there is no doubt that coercion was employed to mobilize manual labour and that this was reinforced through both informal and more official means.[2]

Data on the Zigula people's resistance to forced labour and corvées are interesting because the people living in this area descended from free farmers and former runaway slaves whose origins lay farther south in Bantu-speaking eastern Africa. The WaGosha, as they came to be known, formed one of the most important maroon communities in nineteenth-century eastern Africa. Whilst everyone's ancestry is known to everyone else in the community and has certain social ramifications, the different social status of a person's forebears had little bearing on the Zigulas' agricultural economy, which has been described as 'the nearest thing to a free peasantry that existed in twentieth century Somalia'.[3]

The introduction of forced labour on the expatriate farming concessions had a profoundly negative effect not only on domestic agriculture but also on the local social structure. Although the story of forced labour under the fascist regime 'has not been completely told and we may never be able to document it fully',[4] the data presented here may shed some light on the imagery and representations utilized by the people who experienced forced labour in this specific riverine rural area of Somalia and how this influenced their resistance to it. The data are based on a substantial collection of oral sources gathered in Somalia before the outbreak of civil war at the end of 1990.[5]

Forced to labour

As summarized several years ago by Cassanelli, the problem of availability of wage labour for agricultural work was not resolved after the end of slavery in Somalia when such labour was so important for the agricultural colonization of Somalia.[6] Local farmers saw paid labour as a supplement to their own agricultural activity rather than a substitute for it. Consequently, they were not available for hire during key periods of the agricultural cycle because they had to work their own land, a situation that was prejudicial to the labour requirements of the big landowners. The policy of *compartecipazione* proposed by the agronomist Romolo Onor,[7] suggesting the establishment of concessions with double participation of indigenes and Italians in order to have local people's maintaining vested interest in them, was rejected and agricultural development was to be promoted by means of agricultural concession to Italian expatriates. Thus, out of a range of possible solutions, the option chosen by the fascist ideologue Paolo De Vecchi was the one that had the least likelihood of success though it simultaneously offered the greatest potential for an exhibition of nationalist vainglory.

Between 1920 and 1933 the number of concessions operating in the Italian colony of Somalia rose from four to 115.[8] In the Oltregiuba, the Consorzio della Colonizzazione del Giuba had let approximately 25 concessions which were located between three and 60 kilometres from the river Juba estuary. The total area under expatriate cultivation in this location was approximately 2,500 hectares.[9] The greatest concentration of concessions was located in the zone between the towns of Yontey and Jamaame.

As part of the deal, the Italian government implied that colonists would have access to local labour, in the process underestimating the problems this resolution would create. The settled descendants of ex-slaves and lineages of free agriculturalists were considered more disciplined and much harder workers than Somali pastoralists and were therefore the main targets for conscription into corvées for public utility works. This disrupted their own farming work by releasing some labour to the agricultural concessions and resentment ensued when seasonal flooding or any other natural calamity that affected the concessions was classified as a 'public utility service'. This occurred, for example, along the Shebeli River in 1923, and affected the Società Agricola Italo-Somala directed by the Duca d'Abbruzzi.[10]

According to local inhabitants of the Gosha area in the southern Juba area of Somalia, the Italians began enforcing compulsory labour after the Abyssinian war[11] (Italo-Ethiopic war, 1935–36) and this coercion only lasted for a few years, that is, until the British occupation in 1941.[12] This testimony implies that the practice intensified in the Gosha much later than along the Shebeli River where compulsory labour, coerced through the manipulation of the Bertello contract in the Italian farms, had been enforced for at least the previous decade. Forced labour continued under the BMA, which repatriated some Italian concession-holders from detention camps in Kenya to Somalia in order to reactivate their estates and make them productive.[14]

In the Gosha, the Zigula say that the way that forced labour was implemented fostered very negative feelings of mistrust within their community that persist to the present. At the heart of the system were lists of personnel that were compiled by privileged local leaders at the insistence of the Italian administration. The lists comprised virtually everybody who could work, apart from the elderly and members of the leaders' families, whose exemption from forced labour was a form of informal compensation to local leaders for services rendered to the administration. The selected workers were then allocated to a particular estate, where they worked for five days of the week. They were allowed home at weekends.

This co-option of local leaders did not provide colonists with an assured labour force because they tended to supply lists with a great many omissions. The administration's response was to employ paid informers to report on those people who had not been included in the lists. When found, these so-called missing workers were told that unless they complied with the administration's demands on their labour, their elders would be forced to take their place. Normally, older people were excused from working on the farms. This tactic caused many quarrels and disagreements within the community, as members of the spies' families took revenge on the reluctant workers' families by denouncing them to the authorities.

Having the ability to compile lists of people's names was one thing; it was quite another to compel the people on the list to work in the concessions. Enforcement was neither peaceful nor without victims. For instance, Mame Kajendo Mganga remembered that a group of armed *askari* (African colonial police) called *Banda* was sent to her village, Mugambo, to take the men away to the estates. The men had fled the village and were hiding in the bush and so the women decided to conceal themselves in their huts. The *askari* forcibly entered the huts and attempted to rape the women. Mame Kajendo was pregnant and she fought against being undressed and raped and, therefore, she was beaten. She says she had some difficulties during the baby's birth and ascribes these to the assault. The *askari* also attempted to loot the village. The Zigula men, who were hiding nearby, heard the commotion and returned to the village in an attempt to drive out the *askari*.[15]

A similar sort of surveillance system operated on the concessions. In the estates of the Consorzio di Colonizzazione del Giuba, individual workers were assigned a *posto*, a plot of land to work and a task to be completed by the end of the week. The Consorzio's commissioners, like their counterparts elsewhere, visited the farms in rotation at the end of the week and whipped anyone who had not completed their *posto*.[16] Local foremen were expected to act as informers, identifying anyone who had not completed their assigned tasks within the allotted time in accordance with their contract. A male forced labourer was paid three liras per contract and a female labourer 2.5 liras; both men and women were expected to complete five 'contracts' a week.[17] Some foremen were compassionate and did not like to see their neighbours beaten; others were ready to inform on anyone who had not completed their *posto*. The Consorzio's officers took anyone who had not completed their work, or who showed a reluctance to work, to Jamaame; there they were tied to a pole and left in the sun for up to two hours.[18] One of the most ruthless farm owners, a '*signor* Shafi' who had a concession at Wirkoy village, is still remembered today because he perpetrated so many abuses that he was eventually removed from his post.

The entire process of producing manual labour by recruiting forced labour resulted in generalized reciprocal mistrust within Zigula society. The diffusion of paid informers spread the suspicion that everyone was ready to accuse everyone else of desertion and so people began to keep to themselves. The situation encouraged the spread of individualism within the community because people could no longer trust each other as they remember doing before the advent of colonialism.[19] In Zigula terms, this process sowed *usungu* among the families. *Usungu* is a condition of pain or resentment towards somebody that is described as a genuine, physical condition: my 'belly is hot' towards somebody, I 'feel something that affects me from the stomach to the goiter'. To explain what *usungu* is, people say:

A parent weeps for the death of his child and will have *usungu* for that child. If somebody kills your brother, you will feel *usungu* towards the killer. If you avenge your brother by murdering his killer, the *usungu* will pass over to his brothers.

This is expressed in the Zigula saying: '*Na usungu wa Oduguianga, nani hone uneva nouliha*', that is 'I have *usungu* because of [what happened to] my brother; it will heal when I have done the same',[20] namely, after I get revenge.

The resentments and the lack of reciprocal trust claimed by the Zigula in 1988[21] as created by this process contributed to the disappearance of the mutual assistance association for agricultural work known as *soddon*. The *soddon* in southern Somalia was a form of redistribution of agricultural surplus in exchange for agricultural labour. It constituted a network of social relations governed by strict rules. According to Pietro Barile,[22] among the inhabitants of the riverine areas of the Shebeli River, the *soddon* was a form of free agricultural labour allowed by masters and practised among the slaves of many Somali tribes. A fixed day of the week was given to the slaves to work communally on their own farms. This system conceded a kind of temporary free status to those who practised it and an institutional basis for claiming that free day from the masters. A master prevented a slave from participating in a *soddon* at his peril because he knew that demanding work of his slave on these days could provoke all the members of the *soddon* to revolt. Barile argues that, based on the prescribed freedom days given to the slaves, inclusion in a *soddon* was also one of the strategies used by the masters to prevent slaves from fleeing.

In the Gosha area, the characteristics of the *soddon* were different from elsewhere. It is remembered as a kind of competition among richer cultivators. Agriculturalists formed a group and provided manual labour from their families for a full day's work in each other's fields in turn. Large numbers of workers were needed in the rainy season because weeding large areas of cultivated land rapidly was essential in order not to lose the harvest. It is this ecological pressure that gave impetus to the competition.

The owner of the field being worked on had to provide abundant food for all the workers and in the Gosha it was here that the opportunity arose for competitive displays of prestige and wealth. Field owners competed in their offers of food and gifts for their workers. Someone who redoubled another man's offer was said to be using a *jid goi*, a short cut, in that he deflected workers from their legitimate destination according to the *soddon* rules to his own fields. The *jid goi* competition was such that workers could be lured away from someone's fields several times. The *soddon* also operated as a means of distributing food surpluses – goats, sheep, sesame oil – among the workers on a periodic basis. The redistribution of large quantities of sesame oil or other agricultural products through a *jid goi* was very useful to those families whose crops were not ready to harvest or had failed.

Despite the competition, field owners also benefited from the system. A person who needed products to pay for his own turn of the *soddon* could demand loans from neighbours and in so doing generated relations of reciprocal debit/credit. These relationships were binding; no one could escape them. Failure to respect the rules of the *soddon* resulted in punishment by the community. In fact the rules were taken so seriously that elders referred to the *soddon* as *serikali*, a Kiswahili word meaning government, civil administration and authority.

The introduction of forced labour on the agricultural concessions made it impossible for Zigula farmers to work with their *soddon*. The accompanying redistribution system, the prestige competitions and the public demonstrations of wealth disappeared with it. When forced labour finally ended, the mistrust that had been generated by the colonial policy of co-opting local chiefs prevented people from returning to the *soddon* system.

Ostensibly forced labour was only employed in the farming concessions and in public utility works and workers were drawn from the lists created by local chiefs, as amended by paid informers. In reality, entire African families were taken as workers to an estate – mother, father, children and adolescents. Mothers with young children were told to leave them with another woman who looked after several women's children at once so their mothers were free to work.

Whilst collecting autobiographical material from elderly women who had been children or teenagers at the time of the colony, I was told the following story by Mame Nthukano Mnongerwa:

> I was a child and the wife of the owner had a daughter whose name was Mirella. Five of us girls were given the task of looking after her for a month at a time. I pushed her softly on the swing and pushed more strongly the swing of her sister who was older. Mirella's mother took charge of registering our working days. On weekends Mirella cried and cried that she wanted to keep me on the estate and I was not sent back home with my family like the other workers.[23] Then, especially my girl-friend Fatumo cried, as she wanted to see her family.[24] Mirella only wanted to keep staying with us; she did not realise that we missed our families.

Of course Mirella's mother was probably right in thinking that working as baby sitters was a more appropriate job for teenagers than forced farming. Other women find their memories much harder to bear. The following anec-dote, related to me in 1988 by Mame Keray, illustrates the terrible depres-sion she and other young women felt as a result of the coercive labour system. She had been a teenage wife at the time of the colony and had lost her first three children while she was working on the estates because she was stressed and could not breastfeed them properly.

> We were all working in a rice plantation with our legs in the water, when an airplane flew over our heads. We made a lot of signals to the pilot from land. Later, he landed and came to ask what we wanted from him. We told that we wished him to bomb us so that we would have stopped all our sufferings by dying.[25]

Mame Keray was deeply marked by her experiences of the colonial regime's economic and sexual policies.

Forced marriage

One institution the Italians considered a very effective means of obtaining greater productivity from their coerced labour force is remembered in the oral histories as *nikaax talyaani*, that is, Italian marriage.[26] I have described this elsewhere,[27] but as it can be considered a form of slavery, I think it is relevant to give a brief outline of the practice here.

To provide men with an incentive to work on the Italian farm conces-sions, a colonial law allowed men to choose a woman and marry her without her consent or the agreement of her family. A man describes the way it was:

In the farm where you were conscripted they asked you who you wanted to marry. They prepared lists and shortly afterwards they brought you the woman as a wife ... You could only request one woman and you were not allowed to divorce her. You were both slaves of the estate.[28]

The assumption underpinning this system was that men would have been reluctant to work and more inclined to revolt if they did not have a wife with whom to sleep. Giving men the power to choose a wife without constraints, even if he was only allowed one, was definitely an incentive in a society in which the traditional procedure involved a whole set of agreements between families, a marriage contract and a number of marriage transactions. Preparations for traditional marriages required time and effort on the part of the groom and his family, who had to gather the goods for the ceremony. The new decree swept that all away. All a man had to do was to walk into the Italian Resident's Office, point out the girl he wanted, and she became his wife. However, identifying himself to the Resident meant that the man could no longer escape forced labour.

Many of the girls selected as wives under this system were extremely young. Girls were taken from the ritual seclusion of their initiation into adulthood, before the *buinda* initiatory dance. Mame Nthukano Mnongerwa recalled how she and two other teenage girls were taken from the seclusion of the *buinda* ritual.[29] They were taken to the town of Margherita (Jamaame) to be handed over to the men who had requested them in marriage. As they were *mwali* – in the process of being initiated – their heads and bodies were covered with a white *kaniki*, or cotton cloth. In Margherita, Mame Nthukano was told that five men had chosen her as their wife and it was only when she was in the Resident's presence that he discovered that she was already married to Mze Mnongerwa. The Resident recommended that her husband come to reclaim her as a matter of urgency, otherwise he would give her to another man on the spot. Mame Nthukano was released shortly thereafter.[30] When interviewed in 1988, she was still traumatized by this experience and she was afraid to sing the Fascist song *Faccetta Nera* ('Little Black Face') in front of anyone other than her two brothers. This was among the few Italian songs she knew and she wished to show it to me as a matter of courtesy although the song brought back to her memory a great number of frightening experiences.

Mame Kutukira recalled how she and many other girls who had not yet passed their menarche were taken from home under the pretext of working on the estates. Instead, they came back home 'with the *ndanga* on their heads',[31] that is, wearing the black scarf used by married women.

Indeed, many girls were married before puberty. An elderly Zigula man remembered that, 'Some girls were taken in marriage when they were six or seven years old. There were people who did this to take revenge against their families'.[32] In other words, the decree was utilized by older men as a means of avenging animosities between families:[33] for example, a man would marry a girl who had been refused him and promised to another just to spite the girl's relatives and the promised husband.

In Zigula society, where marital alliances play an important role in settling conflicts and animosities, the sexual slavery enforced by this colonial decree caused great social confusion and profound internal divisions. Male oral sources mention this; only women can tell of the mistreatment and damage they suffered as a result of this decree.

Resisting forced labour

There is no doubt that the period when forced labour was implemented in the Italian colony was strewn with discord and disagreements. The Zigula associate the time with the idea of having fallen back into slavery. In several interviews, individuals recounted their reactions to having been called slaves by either Somalis or colonists. One killed a Somali man for this reason[34] and another was gaoled for a month for assaulting the Italian Resident.

Resistance to forced labour took several forms, though it was generally limited to individual acts. Some people from the Gosha area escaped, separately, to town in order to avoid forced labour; others asked Somali nomads for protection, thus renouncing their freedom.[35] Several people went to prison and many were physically punished for protesting against the practice. One story is recounted of a hero of the resistance called Ali Shora, a Warday man. As his son had been taken away by force to work on the Far Wamo canal, Ali is said to have armed himself with a shield and sword against the master.[36] Sooyan, a *reer*[37] Shabelle local leader of the Ajuraan[38] in the mid-Juba valley, refused to send his people to work in the concessions. His decision led to an invitation to affiliate his people with the Ajuraan people escaping from forced labour in other southern areas of the Juba.[39]

Other local leaders refused to collaborate with the recruitment of forced labour undertaken by the Zigula. According to oral sources, Zigula chiefs were asked by the BMA to recruit workers from villages in the northern areas of the Gosha, towards the villages of Bardera Yerey and Jilib.[40] People remember that one of them, Mze Chibango, resigned from his position as chief during the BMA because he was unwilling to collaborate. Mze Muuse Mberwa was tortured by being placed on a bed of hot gravel and covered with an awning for refusing to supply the required lists of names to the BMA.[41]

Some workers organized protests in which an entire labour unit slackened the pace of their work so that the tasks of a particular day could not be accomplished. To defeat this form of resistance, the Italians encouraged informers and destroyed morale by interviewing every participant individually, thereby discovering the instigators of the stoppage.[42]

An important event of communal resistance to forced labour was a real strike. The narrative of the chief organizer of the protest march, Mze Luhizo Matua,[43] expresses the dynamic created between chiefs paid by the government and other local leaders and explains why the Zigula speak of the community trust that failed and did not re-establish itself with the passing of the colony:

> Nine people gathered in the bush in order to plan how to fight against the colonial regime of forced labour. They decided to speak with the commissioner to argue that the Zigula refused to work in the farms with their wives. It was decided that the three leaders of the action in order of importance were to be Mze Luhizo Matua, Mze Mberwa Sugini and Mze Mamadi Mgaia. The three persons were chosen through a *mnamulo* [act of divination].[44] Mze Luhizo started his trip from the village of Mugambo by blowing and singing a shell like a horn in which some *uganga* [spells] had been placed. He gathered people from the villages of Moofi, Buulo Yaq, Mwasaghiro, Takaungu, and Borini to follow him and went with them to the Italian officer 'Gargarsi'.[45] From the villages of Migwa and Fikiro nobody wanted to follow, but from other villages along the way many people accompanied the strike, also from Kobon and Zunguni. The group that reached Yontey was made of eight to nine hundred adult people – between thirty-eight and sixty years of age[46] – who, together with their wives, all affirmed that they did not want to work for the colony. Gargarsi called the soldiers from Kisimayo. When the demonstrators were in front of the army, Mr. Gargarsi asked who was the leader of the protest and Mze Luhizo advanced saying that the people had come to say that they were not available to work for the colony. The officer put him aside and asked the crowd who agreed with him. After a second request, somebody mediated saying that they wanted houses because they could not work in the farms without roofs under which to sleep. Then the administrator promised that every master would build houses for the workers. Others said that the job to be accomplished at the farms in a day was too much, that is, the amount of land to be weeded was too large. The administrator promised that it would be reduced by half. At this point Gargarsi asked Mze Luhizo whether he intended to continue with his claims. He confirmed that he would not work in the colony in any way and was therefore taken to Kisimayo jail, where he remained for nine days together with Mhamdeni and Hassani who wanted to accompany him.

There are a number of interesting points in this narrative. It is not clear why the account indicates a lack of representatives from the villages of Migwa and Fikiro, although this may be related to long-term disputes between the villages. On the other hand, the presence among the demonstrators of representatives from the villages of Kobon and Zunguni – where the residents are mostly non-Zigula speakers – points to the hegemonic character of this protest for 'freedom' headed by the Zigulas. It is evident that the officer was aware of labourers' complaints regarding inadequate housing and the amount of assigned work and played a paternalist game to divide the demonstrators. The complaint concerning the lack of decent workers' housing was common in many concessions in the Somali colony at the time.[47] Elderly Zigula women told me that in the Juba concessions there was no separate accommodation for male and female workers and that this was very difficult to cope with. Moreover, there was no privacy for married couples and no separate sleeping quarters for younger, unmarried people or those who had not brought their partners with them to the concessions. The inadequate shelter, together with the great social promiscuity in which the labourers were expected to live, reveals the colonists' perception of local farmers as an indistinguishable mass of human labour. Bad working conditions were not, however, the main concerns driving the protest's leaders or even, perhaps of the entire group of demonstrators. Rather, as the Zigula had fought for their freedom from slavery in the preceding decades,[48] the leaders of the protest were much more concerned with freedom from all forms of coercive labour.

Finally, the narrator's emphasis on the fact that demonstrators were men accompanied by their wives is interesting. This is meant to reinforce the idea that Zigula men and women were united in their resistance to forced labour, despite the divisive impact of the *nikax talyaani* on gender relations. Also interesting is the narrator's emphasis on the age range of the participants, which indicates the maturity and responsibility of those who took part. They would have been the parents and grandparents of the young men who were the principal targets of coerced labour and of the young girls the administration had so recklessly disposed of under the 'Italian marriage' decree.

The narrative of the protest march continues with the prosecution of those who had organized it:

> The administrator Mr. Gargarsi called the chief of the *taraf* [administrative unit], Mze Maiange Chipande, and threatened him: should he not find the other people who had organised the strike, it would be assumed he had organised it himself. Mze Maiange looked for those responsible, but nobody admitted responsibility for [organising] the strike. Finally, Mze Luhizo Matua was sent back home. Mze Maiange sent a letter to the Italian administration stating that he could not control the region until Mze Luhizo was free because he [Luhizo] would have spoiled his [Maiange's] work as he [Luhizo] continuously attempted to convince other people to revolt. Thereafter, Mze Luhizo was brought back to Kisimayo jail for two months and, later, was sent to the Hafun prison. Also Mze Mberwa and Mze Mamadi were taken with him as they had been identified as co-organisers of the strike. Mze Luhizo wrote to the government saying that Mze Maiange had participated in the meeting to organise the protest march and that, therefore, he should be sent to court as well. Two years and five months later he received an answer stating that his petition was in court. When the court case finally

reached Mogadishu, the petition became unimportant because the Second World War had begun and Mze Luhizo was sent back home from Mogadishu with the last vessel to Kisimayo.

It is impossible to know how far the claim for freedom would have gone had not the Second World War broken out. During the BMA, the suppression of resistance to the forced labour system was justified by the administration on the grounds that the country was at war and people had to give their support to the war effort. It was a time of great scarcity and people recall having to dress in old sacks[49] for lack of cloth or the money to buy any. Whilst the Italians are blamed for introducing the forced labour system, the British are remembered for not paying for the work done under it – even though BMA documents declare a daily wage of 12 liras for men, eight liras for women and six liras for children.[50]

Local chiefs who were strongly identified with the implementation of the forced labour system and who penalized their neighbours for non-compliance, were anything but highly regarded within their communities. The case recalled by Mze Luhizo highlights the change in loyalty relations resulting from the colonists' policy of giving incentives to individuals or groups such as informers. Apparently, Mze Maiange had been among the first to look for ways of resisting forced labour and mobilizing protestors against it; he knew all about the meeting at which the strike was organized. Nevertheless, he is blamed for not wanting to admit this publicly, for fear of losing the power bestowed on him by the colonists.[51] He had been on the Italians' payroll since at least 1935, when he and other selected/co-opted local leaders received 150 liras a month.[52] Later, in 1937, his particular stipend had increased to 320 liras monthly, half as much again as that of other chiefs of the Margherita Residency. This was a very high wage rise compared with that of the chiefs of the Jilib Residency whose stipend was only raised to 180 liras per month,[53] which seems to suggest the value Italians attributed to chiefs' co-option in the area of Margherita where most of the concessions where located. Mze Maiange is said to have died after a sequence of serious illnesses that people ascribe to the many bad things he had done to his people in his lifetime. Many spells are said to have been cast against him by his own neighbours.

One system used by the colonists to control people was, then, the co-option of their chiefs through payments and the bestowal of privileges. Another common strategy was to target individuals whom they considered unruly and who reacted strongly against the colonists' authority. Such people would be punished for their unruliness and then co-opted into paid work for the colonial authorities in areas where they could be more easily controlled. For instance, one such case was a boy who, after having been punished, was hired and well paid as a boy in the residency of Margherita.

Prestige, power, and unfree labour

Categories like poverty, unfree labour, forced labour, slavery and prestige given by wealth in this specific historic and cultural context have rather shifting meanings. Individuals may rise or fall from one category to another during their lifetime without permanently affecting their vision of life. Working as temporarily unfree, unpaid or scarcely paid labour is not uncommon for people in this area, which is prone to natural disasters, famine and other harsh realities such as war. The climate, with its droughts and floods, can reduce anyone to poverty at any time. In times of severe hardship, the work of one's children, or of the household's teenagers, is sold to someone who needs low cost agricultural labour. This provides the household with some necessary income. In fact, associations such as the *korsaar*, organized by women for agricultural labour purposes, practically institutionalize this practice in order that a mother can produce some income to support the household.[54] This is simply part of the daily life of poor people and is not considered unfair on the children: when there is no other means of obtaining money, occasional daily work is performed by both adults and children. In many instances, people work first and ask for payment later; working without settling the rate for the work in advance allows people to acquire credit for it, which they can claim at a later date. This is why one can see people in difficult times such as famines, for example, working without requesting a specific amount of recompense in advance. At the very least, however, the workers expect payment in food. In other situations, the anticipated return will, of course, be different.

Attitudes towards unfree labour, unpaid labour or exploitative labour can therefore seem fatalistic. However, this apparent indifference conceals expectations of some return in the future. When someone who is a labour-giver, rather than a labour-taker, is satisfied with the prestige of this position at a particular point in time, this is because it is seen as a moment in what is perceived to be a cyclical condition. Two very similar cases, occurring at different times in history, may clarify the extent to which people consider the roles of labour-giver and labour-taker as interchangeable.

The first case concerns a Zigula boy called Awes, who was a young boy during the Italian colony in the Lower Juba. He had refused to work on the farms and was punished for his recalcitrance. Having escaped farm work, he was taken on as a 'boy' (paid domestic servant) by a Mr Costa in Margherita. There Awes witnessed many of the inhumane punishments that were meted out during the colonial period. When the British took over from the Italians in 1941, young Awes decided to avoid the possibility of more forced labour and enrolled in the British army as an *askari*. He was posted to Kenya and served at a detention camp, where he again met Mr Costa, who was then a prisoner of war. Rather than dominating Mr Costa through the same violence the prisoner had used against his people, Awes vaunted his freedom by offering him cigarettes and bringing him things from outside the camp. In other words, he exercised and demonstrated his power benevolently.

The second case is that of a Zigula woman named Amina,[55] whom I met in the early 1990s in Tanzania. She and her children had spent several months in Kisimayo, where they had almost died of starvation. Then she spent two years in the Daddab refugee camp in northeastern Kenya. When I last interviewed her she was earning about US$40 a month in Dar es Salaam and supporting five children and two adults. She described what she had to do to feed her children and survive Kisimayo. She began working for ethnic Somalis living in town who were richer at the time. She cleaned the house, did the dishes and the laundry. Sometimes she would be paid in staple foods; sometimes she was given the leftovers from the family's meals; and sometimes, after she had finished all her assignments, they would say they had nothing to give her. After some months of this, she and her husband realized they would all die of starvation in these conditions and so they decided that Amina and the smaller children should go to a refugee camp in Kenya. Because they were considered vulnerable (to rape and starvation), Amina and the children were sent to Dabbab refugee camp. Two years later, she was relatively well placed in the camp, insofar as one can be in such sort of accommodation. She was working as a social worker and was responsible for a quarter of the camp. A number of Somalis began arriving as new refugees from Kisimayo with neither money nor food, among them people who had been rich but who, because of the political changes in the town, had fallen into poverty. The man who had employed Amina in Kisimayo was just such a refugee. He came to her to ask for help, in remembrance of the fact that she had worked in his house and therefore had been previously somewhat helped by him. In other words, this previous relationship implied some sort of social obligation. Rather than being resentful or vengeful for the many times he had sent her home without food after a full day's work, she demonstrated her new power by sending him to somebody who could help him. In presenting herself as powerful and benevolent, she was displaying not only her power but also her prestige.

The question here is what is the rationale that pushed two different people to behave in the same way in different contexts at different times? It seems likely, in this cultural context, that both Awes and Amina perceived poverty as something that was brought about by unforeseeable circumstances that could affect anybody at any time. In such circumstances accepting an offer of unfree and exploitative work was simply a matter of survival. They also appear to have believed that the unforeseeable circumstances that reduced them to poverty could just as unpredictably change their fortunes for the better. Both Awes in the 1940s and Amina in the 1990s experienced the unpredictability of life, plunging them into poverty. Neither of them, however, developed a strong wish for revenge, let alone the usual claim on the wealth that people often feel has been accumulated behind their backs when witnessing big differences in living standards. In both cases, the economic and social privileges of the oppressors do not seem so crystallized in the essence of people belonging to a particular clan, class, ethnic, racial or skin colour category. Rather, both Awes and Amina found it more satisfying to demonstrate their dominant status benevolently rather than by exacting revenge against their former oppressors. Perhaps they considered it more profitable in the long run to ensure the benevolence of their former oppressors in order to acquire 'credits' from them for future use should the wheel of fortune turn again.

In Somalia, political history moves fast. People who were rich before the recent civil war (from 1990 onwards) became poor as a result. That some people consider it a more sensible strategy to play their dominant positions by offering help and giving advice rather than exacting revenge probably stems both from the fact that there is no fixed or codified social stratification based on long accumulated economic wealth and from the cultural expectation of delayed returns on credits acquired.

Concluding considerations

Forced labour in this area of Somalia, despite being described by the Zigula who experienced it as a condition similar to the earlier slavery, was actually more pernicious than slavery. In the nineteenth century and by the beginning of the twentieth, being labelled slaves and/or having a common past of slavery had fostered unity and the shaping of a common identity in the Gosha,[56] yet the way coercive labour was enforced by both the Italian and British administrations proved to be particularly disruptive of the social networks on which the community was based. Forced labour undermined the social dynamics that had helped the communities of descendants of runaway and freed slaves to rebuild their identity in the nineteenth century on a unified and defensive strategy against the surrounding Somalis who had attempted to regain mastery over them.

Italian colonial policy sought to control communities through co-opting local leaders by paying them to act against their own villages and friends. It sought to control individuals through the enforced submission of individual women to individual men in 'Italian marriage'. The latter policy, designed to ensure that men would work on the farming concessions, greatly empowered men by upsetting established social relations among matrikin groups as well as hierarchical authority within individual families. The 'Italian marriage' allowed young boys to modify long-term family relationships and gave older men the opportunity to avenge old animosities.

Resistance was organized by local leaders who resigned, by individuals who refused to work, by women who escaped from rape, and by people who organized protest marches and were punished for it. Other people collaborated with the foreign authorities. Some were cruel and enjoyed the potential for vengeance; others were more benign. Some men welcomed the ability to choose a wife through the 'Italian marriage' system not least because organizing a traditional marriage was incompatible with the obligations of forced labour. Young women and girls were not in a position to resist these marriages and were co-opted or abducted into unwanted marriages, their extreme youth, workload and the obstacles interposed to breast-feeding leading to the loss of many of their children. The trauma of the situation was still very much alive in the memories of the people I interviewed in 1988.[57]

Notes

* Many thanks to all those Zigulas who collaborated with my research work, recounting and making their historical memories available to me.

1 G. Salvadei, 'Contro il lavoro coatto nelle colonie', *L'Oltremare*, 8. 5 (1934), pp. 169–72.

2 Angelo Del Boca, A., *Gli Italiani in Africa Orientale, 2: La Conquista dell'Impero* (Milano: Laterza, 1986), pp. 203–5.

3 Lee V. Cassanelli, 'The End of Slavery and the 'Problem' of Rural Labour in Colonial Somalia', in Annarita Puglielli (ed.), *Proceedings of the Third International Congress of Somalia Studies* (Roma: Il Pensiero Scientifico Editore, 1986), p. 273.

4 Ibid. p. 278.

5 The cataloguing system of the sources is explained in Francesca Declich, 'Two Hundred Years along the Juba River: Gendered Narratives, History and Identity among the Zigula and Shanbara', *History in Africa*, 22 (1995), p. 1.

6 Cassanelli, 'The Ending of Slavery in Italian Somalia: Liberty and the Control of Labor, 1890–1935', in Suzanne Miers and Richard Roberts (eds), *The End of Slavery in Africa* (Madison, University of Wisconsin Press, 1988), pp. 308–31.

7 Romolo Onor, *La Somalia Italiana. Esame critico dei problemi di economia rurale e di politica economica della colonia* (Torino: Fratelli Bocca, 1925).

8 Cassanelli, 'The End of Slavery', p. 276; Robert L. Hess, *Italian Colonialism in Somalia* (Chicago: University of Chicago Press, 1966).

9 O. A. Spencer, 'A Survey of agriculture in Somalia with Special Reference to the Irrigated Schemes of the Juba and Webi Shebeli valleys', 28 May 1943: Public Record Office (hereafter PRO), Kew, Foreign Office (hereafter FO) 1015/73.

10 Del Boca, *Gli Italiani in Africa*, 2: p. 83.

11 Fieldnotes (1988), va3: 76, Fieldnotes (1988) o/sto: 38 and Fieldnotes (1988), o/sto: 62.

12 Fieldnotes (1988), o/sto: 23.

13 Del Boca, *Gli Italiani in Africa*, 2: pp. 83, 203; M. Serrazanetti, *Considerazioni sulla nostra attività coloniale in Somalia*, (Bologna: Istituto Agronomico dell'Oltremare, Tipografia La Rapida, 1933)

14 'Agricultural Advances, To: M. J. Stewart, Col.', 23 January 1945: PRO, FO 1015/73; Declich, *I Bante della Somalia: Etnogenesi e rituali mviko* (Milano: Franco Angeli, 2002), pp. 136–7.

15 Fieldnotes (1988), tr2: 50–1, 69–71.

16 Fieldnotes (1988), o/sto: 64.

17 Fieldnotes (1988), tr1: 33–5.

18 Fieldnotes (1988), o/sto: 61; o/sto: 63.

19 Fieldnotes (1988), o/sto: 56.

20 Fieldnotes (1988), o/sto: 55.

21 Fieldnotes (1988), o/sto: 56.

22 Pietro Barile, *Colonizzazione fascista nella Somalia Meridionale* (Roma: Società Italiana di Arti Grafiche, 1935).

23 Fieldnotes (1988), tr4: 46–50, 61–2; Fieldnotes (1988) o/sto: 21.
24 Fieldnotes (1988), o/sto: 21.
25 Fieldnotes (1988), tr1.
26 Fieldnotes (1988), o/sto: 120, Fieldnotes (1988), o/sto: 120, Kenneth Menkhaus, 'Rural Transformation and the Root of Underdevelopment in Somalia'a Lower Jubba Valley', University of South California, PhD thesis (1989), p. 259.
27 Declich, 'Two Hundred Years along the Juba River' and *I Bante della Somalia*, pp. 132–4.
28 Fieldnotes (1988), p/sto: 65.
29 For description of the ritual see Declich, *I Bante della Somalia*, pp. 207–12.
30 Fieldnotes (1988), tr4: 51–3.
31 Fieldnotes (1988) tr2: 49.
32 Fieldnotes (1988), o/sto: 65.
33 Fieldnotes (1988), o/sto: 65.
34 Fieldontes (1988), o/sto: 103.
35 Menkhaus, 'Rural Transformation', p. 262.
36 Fieldnotes (1988), o/sto: 25.
37 *Reer* is a Somali word used in different ways. In this case, it refers to people bound by the patriclan Shabelle.
38 The Ajuraan are a branch of the Haawiye clan who established their rule over the inter-riverine region of Somalia during the sixteenth and seventeenth centuries in Virginia Luling, *Somali Sultanate. The Geledi City-State over 150 Years* (London: Haan, 2002), p. 17.
39 British colonial documents from Wajir District (KNA, 1938) in Catherine Besteman, *Unraveling Somalia. Race, Violence, and the Legacy of Slavery* (Philadelphia: University of Pennsylvania Press, 1999), pp. 88–9.
40 Fieldnotes (1988).
41 Fieldnotes (1988), o/sto: 99.
42 Menkhaus, 'Rural Transformation', pp. 262–3.
43 This case is also discussed in Declich, *I Bante della Somalia*, pp. 129–32
44 Words in square brackets are the author's translations.
45 This is the local pronunciation of an Italian surname.
46 Some accounts say the demonstrators numbered 2,600 people. Fieldnotes (1988) o/sto: 23.
47 Franco Monile, *Somalia (Ricordi e visioni)* (Bologna: Licinio Cappelli, 1932), pp. 108–11, in Del Boca, *Gli Italiani in Africa Orientale*, 2: p. 89.
48 Declich, *I Bante della Somalia*, pp. 110–25.
49 Fieldnotes (1988), o/sto: 107.
50 Spencer, 'A survey of agriculture'.
51 Fieldnotes (1988), va3.
52 Decreto Governatoriale n. 11092 del 28 settembre 1935–XIII.
53 Decreto Governatoriale n. 12938 dell'8 settembre 1937–XV.
54 Declich, 'Groups of Mutual Assistance: Masculine and Feminine Agricultural Work among Agriculturalists along the Juba River,' *Northeast African Studies*, 4, 3 (1997), pp. 77–89.
55 Amina is not her true name to avoid any harm this evidence could provoke.
56 Declich, *I Bante della Somalia*.
57 Information for this study is based on fieldwork carried out between 1985 and 1988 comprising ethnographic data and oral histories in the form of individual and 'group' reminiscences, and autobiographical material.

4   Forced labour and the 1856 revolt on Mayotta

Isabelle Denis

Introduction

In the early nineteenth century, Mayotta, the southernmost of the Comoro Islands situated at the northern end of the Mozambique Channel between the east African mainland and Madagascar, served as a depot for slaves exported from East Africa. From the 1820s, it also became a refuge for Sakalava from northwest Madagascar fleeing raids launched by the Merina of the high central plateau. Fear of the Merina caused the population of Mayotta to appeal for French protection in 1841 and in 1843 the island became a French colony. The French hoped that Mayotta would compensate them for the loss of Mauritius, seized by the British during the Napoleonic Wars and, unlike neighbouring Réunion island, not returned in the Peace settlement of 1814. The British retained Mauritius because it possessed in Port Louis a major port and dockyard, whereas Réunion possessed no good harbours. The French thus hoped that Mayotta, which had a good natural harbour, would give them an Indian Ocean naval base close to the major east African entrepôt of Zanzibar, where the Americans and British traders were dominant, and to Madagascar, to which the French had colonial claims.

In the mid-nineteenth century, the French islands of the south-west Indian Ocean possessed plantation economies cultivating mainly exotic produce for sale in Europe.[1] Traditionally, these plantations were worked by slaves. Slavery was progressively abolished, in British colonies between 1834 and 1838 and in French territories from 1847–48, although a clandestine slave trade continued both to the plantation islands and to the Americas.[2] The French government quickly surveyed the economic potential of Mayotta and decided to transform it into a plantation economy. They had had considerable experience of managing plantations in the region, and of dealing with slavery and revolts such as occurred in Saint-Denis in the early 1830s. However, Mayotta formed an exception in that slavery was abolished there in 1847, a year before abolition in other French colonies, because the French officers stationed at Saint-Denis, on the nearby island of Réunion, were strongly influenced by the anti-slavery sentiments of the Saint-Simonian school. In this context, the revolt of March to April 1856, involving workers on a number of plantations, came as a surprise.

This chapter examines the basic causes of the Mayotta revolt, notably the system of agricultural concessions practised there and an associated growth in forced labour. It analyses how these caused rising resentment in a population that in 1841 had accepted the French presence to offer them protection against Merina aggression. Finally, it looks at the suppression of the 1856 revolt and its consequences; the creation of a colony of exploitation, open to 'development' by Réunion and French-based companies and merchants.

The concession system

The 1841 treaty failed to provide clear lines as to land ownership and use on Mayotta. While declaring the general principle of recognition of the property rights of the indigenous population, it proclaimed government ownership of all uncultivated land, and introduced the idea both of requisition without indemnity and of obliging the local population to occupy and farm uncultivated terrain.

From 1845, the French authorities implemented a system of granting land to French settlers on terms whereby the concessionaire was obliged to bring the land under cultivation within a five-year period. Given tropical conditions, this could prove difficult on previously uncultivated land, but settlers were given the option of negotiating to take over indigenous fields. Those that did were also obliged by the authorities to cultivate food crops, because the indigenous population no longer possessed sufficient land to cultivate their own. However, it was uncertain precisely what the obligation to assign a portion of land for the cultivation of subsistence crops implied.[3]

The first French companies on Mayotta, the Nantes firms of Ciret and Armanet, already possessed Indian Ocean interests. Ciret established itself in Kaweni, a natural cirque to the north of Mamoudzou, immediately opposite Dzaoudzi, the main port located on the small island called Petite Terre. Proximity to the port facilitated the export of their produce. Armanet established itself in the large and calm Longoni Bay just to the north of Kaweni. Each of the companies was accorded the maximum concession of 500 hectares. Many smaller planters also obtained concessions, notably at Soulou to the west and at Passamainti and Ajangua to the east and by 1856 all coastal lands had been granted to foreign concessionaires (Figure 4.1).

This encouraged European settlers to pressurize indigenous farmers to hand over more land, and to substitute the cultivation of cash crops for food crops. The French authorities backed the settlers, first conducting a census of all indigenous proprietors, and in 1852 'inviting' the local population to clear and plant previously uncultivated terrain. This measure appears to have had considerable success in the south and west of the island.[4] In 1853, the French decided to re-group the entire indigenous population living outside

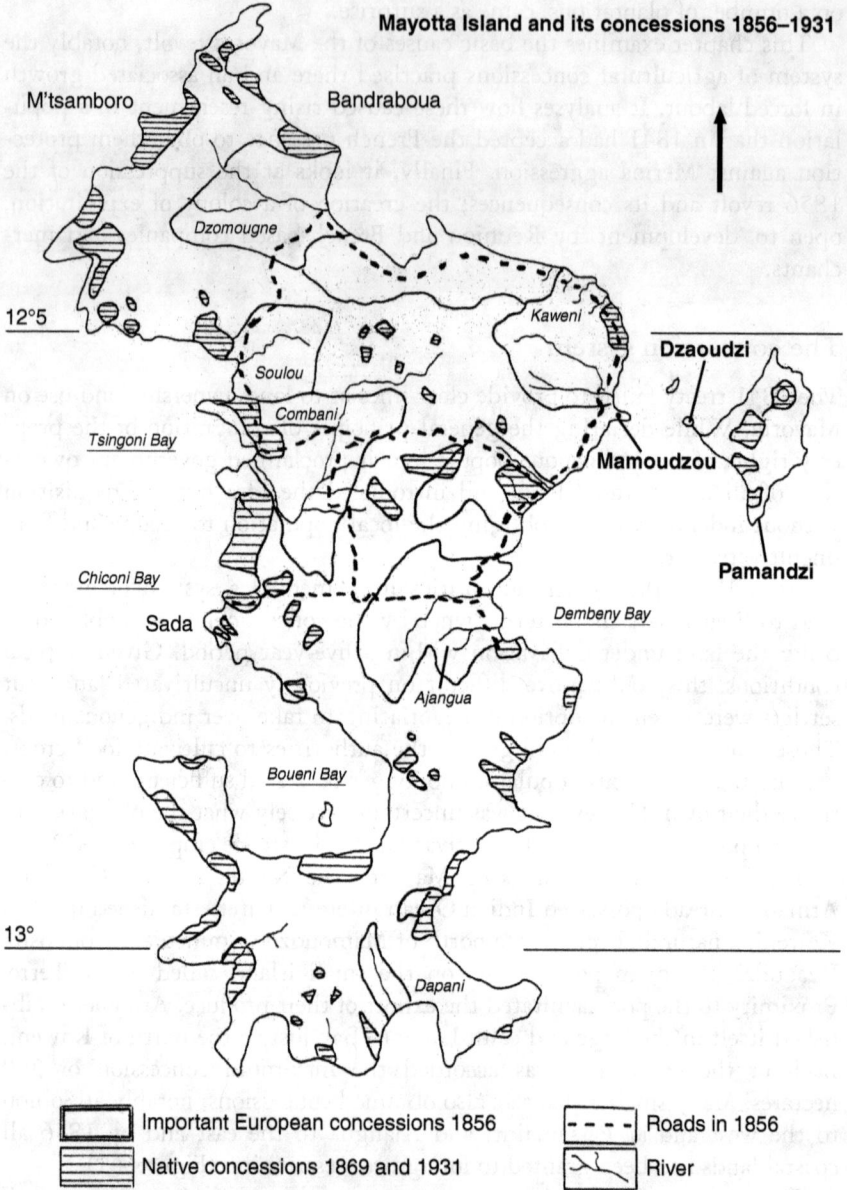

Figure 4.1 Mayotta island and its concessions 1856–1931.

Mayotta Island and its concessions 1856–1931

M'tsamboro

Bandraboua

Dzomougne

12°5

Kaweni

Dzaoudzi

Soulou

Combani

Mamoudzou

Tsingoni Bay

Pamandzi

Chiconi Bay

Sada

Dembeny Bay

Ajangua

Boueni Bay

13°

Dapani

Important European concessions 1856

Roads in 1856

Native concessions 1869 and 1931

River

European concessions in 191 villages, each under a chief, and strategically located in areas the authorities wished to transform into plantations.[5]

Plantation labour

The end to freedom of residence for the indigenous population also signalled the start of mass forced labour. The planters requested that the authorities grant them a ready supply of cheap labour. Their viewpoint, shared by the authorities, was that the local Mayotta population was intrinsically lazy, preferring a simple life of tropical leisure and surviving on fruit, roots and fish, to wage labour. Consequently, the authorities took action to induce people to work on the plantations. The first such measure in 1851 was to condemn all convicted of vagrancy to public works or to plantation work, on pain of being evicted from the island.[6] When this failed to force sufficient workers onto the plantations, a new and more drastic step was taken. Ex-slaves, liberated in 1847, after the payment of a total of 461,000 francs in compensation to their local owners, were obliged to work on settler plantations. All 2,733 ex-African slaves were forced into five-year contracts, whereby they were paid a monthly wage of 2.5 to three francs, as opposed to the 15 francs received by other labourers.[7]

Such labour sources proved insufficient to satisfy settlers' requirements, so the authorities attempted also to recruit 'free' contract workers from East Africa. For example, in 1849 the French naval ship *l'Eglée*, under Captain Leclerc, negotiated successfully at Zanzibar for 24 labourers who on Mayotta were allocated to the French company Ciret.[8] As too few French ships could be spared for this covert slave trade, the authorities opened it up to local dhow owners and as a result recruitment of East African workers increased. Planters rarely contributed to the costs of the operation which were sometimes partly subsidized by the administration on Mayotta.[9]

In addition, planters received from the colonial budgetary reserves a total of 15,000 francs specifically to enable them to recruit a local Comorian workforce. Comorian sultans were paid 80 francs for every worker they supplied on five-year contracts (compared with ten-year contracts for African immigrant workers). In 1853 and 1854 respectively, Ciret obtained 50 and 257 and Sohier de Vaucouleur, another company, 22 and 101 workers each. In 1855 alone, a total of 822 workers were recruited to work on six plantations. The planters justified this recruitment by claiming it would counter the natural tendency of Comorians to be lazy, and would suppress vagrancy.[10] From 1851, all those who did not possess and work an agricultural plot could be termed vagabonds and either expelled from the island or subjected to forced labour for the government.[11]

Initially, regulations were put in place to protect contract workers. The legislation (*arrêté*) of 18 March 1846 was extended by that of 12 January 1848. Contracts were to be limited to five years and transport costs to be paid by the concessionaire. Each worker was to be given adequate housing and a daily ration of 800 grams of rice, 22 grams of salt and 1.1 kilograms of wood (children under ten years old received half a ration). Working conditions were also regulated, pregnant woman and young mothers being obliged to undertake only light work. Working hours were to be between sunrise and sunset (6 am to 6 pm) with breaks for a midday meal and during very hot periods. No work was to be performed on Sundays (a concession granted in France only from 1906) or public holidays. Monthly wages were to be paid before witnesses and the colonial authorities reserved the right of inspection. These were innovative regulations, the foundations of the first real labour legislation.[12]

The 1856 revolt

What then explains the revolt of March–April 1856? Two of the chief reasons were the non-application of the legislation, and the failure of the authorities to listen to a succession of complaints alleging abuse of the contract system. In 1846, for instance, 37 workers on the Armanet concession lodged a complaint of ill-treatment. Commandant Pierre Passot, who was very close to business interests on the island, concluded that the complaint was groundless and condemned four of the plaintiffs to one month's hard labour for the government. This punishment, imposed in an attempt to dissuade workers from complaining, had no legal basis.[13] Again, in 1852, workers from the Ciret plantation at Kaweni complained that they had not received their salaries,[14] an allegation used the following year by the Sultan of Anjouan as the reason for refusing to send newly recruited workers to that plantation. In 1853 a complaint was also lodged by an islander because he had not been compensated for the seizure of his land, even though it was under cultivation at the time it was taken.[15] Unusually, he won his case as, in 1854, the administrative council adopted by four to two the principle of compensation for cultivated land requisitioned by planters.[16]

In 1855, conditions worsened on the plantations. A notable case was that of the Parisian merchant, Armand Dupérier, who zealously sought to repress local 'vagrancy', failed to pay workers' salaries and used excessive corporal punishment. Complaints increased, but planters practising abuses were seldom forced to pay the prescribed fines (varying from five to ten francs). André César Vérand, Commanding Officer on Mayotta from 1854, attempted to calm affairs through a decree (the arrêté of the 2 October 1855)[17] imposing forced labour contracts of from three to five years on all islanders and forbidding workers who lodged complaints of abuse from leaving their work without authorization.[18]

In 1856, revolt erupted on Mayotta after Vérand sailed to Nosy Be to investigate an attack on a plantation supervisor there by three men armed with spears. On 18 March, between 500 and 600 Sakalava and Mozambicans stopped work and, armed with arrows and spears, fled to the mountains, killing two workers who attempted to resist them. In the mountains, they lit fires to summon the rebels into groups. The authorities attempted to negotiate with them through intermediaries respected by both sides; Paulin Ciret and Léopold Joseph Sohier de Vaucouleur, owners of the oldest concessions, and village chiefs like Nam Po Ko, a Mozambican. A curfew was imposed and a military detachment of 40 men posted to Mamoudzou to await orders. The tension increased from the 3 April with the return of Vérand who abandoned negotiations, imposed a state of siege and demanded troop reinforcements from Réunion. He also refused to modify plantation working conditions for those who returned to work.

On 21 April, two military expeditions were launched against the insurgents, one passing through Passamainti and the centre of the island towards Combani and the mountains, and the other to the north against Dzomougné. In the process, seven rebels were killed, one wounded and 23 taken prisoner. On 3 May a further expedition was launched against the south, reputedly the centre of the insurrection. This time, different tactics were adopted: in three days, 110 people were taken prisoner and such was the atmosphere of intimidation that with the approach of Ramadan and the rice harvest, many insurgents returned to their villages.[19]

The fallout from the revolt

On 2 June, a week-long judicial enquiry was inaugurated and on 21 June the recommended punishments officially proclaimed by the administrative council. The impartiality of certain members of the council was suspect: for example, Theodore Hallez, a judge, and Joseph Gallas, a Marine captain, both members of the council, the following year obtained concessions of respectively 500 and 196 hectares.[20] Justice was rapidly enforced. Bakari Koussou, considered to have been the instigator of the revolt, was proclaimed a traitor and on 22 June publicly executed on the jetty between Dzaoudzi and Pamandzi. Most of the 19 other rebels convicted for armed insurrection and pillage were granted imperial clemency and, rather than being despatched to the penal colony in French Guyana, condemned to several years hard labour on Réunion. Two of the condemned had previously fled to their home island of Nosy Lava, from where they had been recruited as contract workers for Mayotta. However, in 1857 they were caught, handed over by the Queen of Nosy Lava to the French authorities and convicted.[21]

In 1841, the French Navy had aspired to create a new style of colony on Mayotta, but by 1856 it was obvious that such an attempt had failed. By then, most of the island's population had joined the ranks of foreign contract workers in being obliged to perform forced labour. Those who refused to work on plantations were subject to disciplinary measures, including labour in public works in different parts of the island: 30 men were thus employed on the main road to the important northern plantation of Dzomougné.[22] Moreover, working conditions failed to improve. In 1860, the two commanding officers noted many irregularities on the plantations. In order to avoid worker dissent, the colonial administration offered provisions for workers on the larger plantations; for example, it supplied 5,000 kilograms of rice to Sohier de Vaucouleur and 20 carriage cows to Cambourg. Generally, however, worker dissatisfaction grew largely because smaller planters, such as Benjamin Bédier, Marcel Toudic and Ernest Vignerie, constrained by a paucity of funds, paid out monthly wages some four to five months after they were due. Those workers whose contracts ended were often obliged to remain on the plantation in the hope of receiving back wages: 305 men were in this situation on 26 December 1860.

How could calm be maintained when working conditions in the colony steadily deteriorated? The first official steps towards alleviating the situation came in 1868. That year, Auguste Gevrey, the new public prosecutor, proved critical of the existing authorities' punitive approach to those contract labourers, including 27 Kaweny plantation workers, who were jailed for their refusal to work and who, upon their release, resisted efforts to force them back to the plantations. While the commanding officer recommended renewed jail terms and fines, Gevrey demonstrated that there were good reasons for worker dissatisfaction. The 1846 and 1848 laws concerning work conditions had never been applied, so that labourers worked 13 hours a day without breaks or food. They were given unhusked rice, while any pause in work was judged to be a case of 'absenteeism' and punished by a two-day reduction in wages. Moreover, wages were paid irregularly and sometimes in kind, in the form of second-rate goods. Finally, although the 'bar of Justice' ('Barre de justice') had been officially banned in 1867, it continued to be widely used to beat workers.[23]

Thanks to the intervention of Gevrey, worker strikes on the Debeny, Iconi and Loujani plantations were peacefully resolved. Moreover, an open revolt by 200 workers on the Soulou plantation ended bloodlessly, and failed to spread because after the 1856 revolt workers were obliged to live in villages on the plantations to which they were assigned, and thus found it exceptionally difficult to communicate with workers on other plantations.

Following the 1856 revolt, few of the indigenous elite remained. In 1857, seven leading Mayotta citizens requested a concession of 210 hectares for grazing and for the cultivation of food crops. Ten foreign planters petitioned against this request, claiming that it would hinder colonization. Unexpectedly, Vérand judged the petition to be unjust and advocated the allocation of plantations to the local elite free of charge, although his fellow superior officers supported the petitioners so that in 1861 there remained only one indigenous concessionaire, Said Omar, who possessed a 55-hectare plantation. It should be noted that Said had considerable political influence on the other three islands of the Comoro archipelago.[24]

Most European concessions from 1869 to 1931 were located in northern Mayotta, north of the line between Ajangua and Sada, and occupied the entire eastern littoral from the Bandraboua headland to Dembeny Bay, where the Dzomougné and Kaweni plantations were situated (see Figure 4.1). Their relations with the authorities were close, which helped should there arise the need to call for military aid. Also, merchant ships anchored off the east coast, facilitating for the planters there the embarkation of coffee, sugar and perfume plants and disembarkation of imported goods. European farmers further occupied the western littoral between M'stang-amouji and Sada, a coast that possessed wide bays and large fields close to the western portion of the lagoon. There, the two main plantations were those of Soulou and Combani.

Postscript

Only a few large plantations, notably Dzomougné, Kaweni, Soulou and Combani, ultimately prospered. The others failed to survive the economic recession of the 1920s and 1930s and were subdivided in favour of local farmers who gained many small coastline plantations in northern Mayotta. Few European concessions were requested in southern Mayotta because of its mountainous relief and lack of roads, except in Dapani, in the far south. Thus from 1869 and 1931 most of southern Mayotta was divided into small indigenous plots. Amoro, close to the harbour, was the only European plantation in the southeast of the island. At the start of the twentieth century, some indigenous plantations were also established on the small island of Pamandzi, formerly reserved as a 'garden' for the Navy, but were under strict government supervision. At the same time, small indigenous farms were established in the north, centre and south of the island – the origin of the modern small market gardens.[25]

The plantation system changed little over time, while the labour recruitment remained much the same until 1945. Labour shortages were characteristic first of the economy of Mayotta, and subsequently of the rest of the archipelago and of Madagascar when they became French colonies after 1896.[26] Colonial groupings established in Paris pushed for solutions to the labour crisis and for means to promote the economic development of the island: as a result, labour was recruited on the east African coast and in India until the 1920s.[27] The French Navy, which had until the 1870s concurred with the British that dhow shipments of labour from East Africa to the Comoros was a disguised form of the slave trade, continued to monitor dhow movements. Local revolts on the other islands, such as occurred on Anjouan in 1891, due to similar discontent amongst workers and indigenous people, obliged the French authorities to deport the prisoners to neighbouring islands; and, following two revolts on Moheli, in 1899 and 1902, rebel prisoners were sent . . . to Mayotta.

Notes

1 F. Celimene, *L'Economie de l'esclavage colonial* (Paris: CNRS éditions, 2002).
2 W. G. Clarence-Smith, *The Economics of the Indian Ocean Slave Trade, in the Nineteenth Century* (London: Frank Cass, 1989).
3 'Royal Ordinance' (21 October 1845), MAD 242/538. Archives d'outremer (C.A.O.M.), Aix-en-Provence.
4 Commandant Philibert Bonfils, 'letter' (15 October 1852), MAD 235/514, C.A.O.M.
5 Commandant Philibert Bonfils, 'letter' to the Ministry of the Navy and the Colonies (25 February 1853), MAD 235/514, C.A.O.M.
6 Armand Duperrier, 'note' to the 'Director of the Colonies' (14 February 1855), MAD 235/514, C.A.O.M.
7 Arrêté' (9 July 1847), GEN 135/1149, C.A.O.M.
8 Captain Louis Leclerc, 'letter' to the Ministry of the Navy and the Colonies (4 June 1849), MAD 235/514, C.A.O.M.
9 Paulin Ciret, 'letter' to the Ministry of the Navy and the Colonies (8 April 1852), MAD 235/514, C.A.O.M.
10 Armand Duperrier, 'note' to the 'Director of the Colonies' (14 February 1855), MAD 235/514, C.A.O.M.
11 Philibert Bonfils, 'letter' to the Minister of the Navy and the Colonies (25 September 1851), MAD 235/514, C.A.O.M.
12 Legislation governing the recruitment of 'free' workers on Mayotta, MAD 235/514, C.A.O.M.
13 Pierre Passot, 'letter' to the Minister of the Navy and the Colonies (6th August 1846), MAD 235/514, C.A.O.M.
14 Bonfils, 'letter' to Paulin Ciret 6 April 1852, MAD 235/514, C.A.O.M.
15 Sadik ali el Mindi, 'letter' to the Ministry of the Navy and the Colonies (14 August 1853), MAD 250/462, C.A.O.M.
16 Extract from the Legal Proceedings (19 October 1854), MAD 242/538.
17 'Arrêté' (2 October 1855), MAD 273/620, C.A.O.M.
18 'Decree' (5 March 1856), MAD 235/514, C.A.O.M.
19 'Letters' to the Ministry of the Navy and the Colonies relative to the insurrection and condemnation of the rebels, MAD 230/496, C.A.O.M.
20 Mme Marie-Emilie Gallas, 'letter' to the Ministry of the Navy and the Colonies (17 October 1868), MAD 250/562, C.A.O.M.
21 The Governor, 'letter' no. 59 to the Ministry of the Navy and the Colonies (20 April 1857), MAD 230/496, C.A.O.M.
22 André César Vérand, 'letter' to the Ministry of the Navy and the Colonies (1 August 1857), MAD 235/514, C.A.O.M.
23 Minutes of the Mayotta 'Tribunal de 1er instance' (1st semester, 1868), MAD 235/514, C.A.O.M.
24 Extract from the 'rapport de remise de service du commandant Vérand' (10 December 1857), MAD 242/538, C.A.O.M.
25 Maps of the agricultural concessions on Mayotta, 1869 and 1931, MAD 242/539, C.A.O.M.
26 Reports of 'Union coloniale', section Madagascar (1912–1935), 100 APOM (code for the archives of the 'Comité central français pour l'outremer') 520/526/532, C.A.O.M.
27 Ibid.

5 Unfree labour, slavery and protest in imperial Madagascar

Gwyn Campbell

Introduction

During the nineteenth-century Merina Empire in Madagascar, virtually the entire non-elite population were subjected to some degree of unfree labour, either as slaves or as victims of *fanompoana*, or unremunerated forced labour for the Merina state and ruling elite. Both forms of unfree labour (slave and *fanompoana*) were subjected to forms of exploitation against which they protested. Moreover, some forms of protest against 'unfree' labour became infused with ethnic (anti-Merina) and political (anti-imperialist) sentiment. With illustrations drawn from nineteenth-century Malagasy proverbs,[1] this chapter analyses the nature of unfree labour (including slavery) in imperial Madagascar, outlines the main forms of protest against such labour and examines the way in which some of it was channelled into political protest.

The imperial Merina economy

The balance of the factors of production in nineteenth-century Madagascar, as in continental Africa, was characterized by a lack of capital and labour, and plentiful land resources.

The Britanno-Merina alliance of 1820, out of which developed an ambitious project of rapid economic development, promised to alter that: a ban was imposed on the export of slaves who were instead directed into the domestic economy, and British agricultural advisers and artisans were employed to stimulate cash crop and craft production. Also a standing army was formed under British military officers with the intention of rapidly expanding the Merina dominion from a small essentially landlocked region of the central highlands into an island empire and major Indian Ocean power. At the same time, the government of Mauritius promised to compensate the Merina crown in cash and goods for the loss of revenue occasioned by the slave export ban.

For reasons more fully explained elsewhere, the alliance became strained and in 1825–26 the Merina rejected what they considered to be British imperial pretensions and inaugurated an autarkic regime that sought not only to create an island empire, and develop cash crop plantations, but also to enlarge the scope of manufacturing from a craft to an industrial scale focusing on the creation of an armaments industry.[2] Deprived of foreign investment, the Merina regime chose to base its drive for military supremacy and economic development on labour. As a consequence, it moved to secure monopoly control over its labour resources and establish structures to assemble and if necessary train labour, and subsequently to allocate tasks and supervise the workforce.

Two such frameworks for the manipulation of labour emerged. The first and simplest was control over slave labour. Until the early 1850s a series of military expeditions despatched from Imerina enslaved thousands of non-Merina. These were supplemented, and from the 1850s replaced, by predominantly Makua slave imports from East Africa. Until the mid-1820s, and for a brief interlude of prosperity in the 1860s and early 1870s, increased slave supplies benefited all classes of Merina society, but generalized impoverishment of small farmers from *c.*1825–61 and again from the late 1870s to 1896, when the French abolished slavery, led to a concentration of slave ownership in the hands of the ruling elite. Until mid-century, some slaves, notably from the southeast of the island, were channelled into plantation labour on the east coast. However, the majority of slaves served the Merina elite as herders (the cattle and meat trade to the Mascarenes and the export of hides to the United States and Europe were very profitable), field labourers, domestic servants and porters (a court cartel formed to monopolize porterage of freight and passengers within the empire).[3]

The use of slaves predominantly to sustain the Merina elite in luxury, and the Merina fear of slave revolt (for a brief period in the early 1820s all non-Merina males captured in military expeditions were executed to prevent the possibility of a slave rebellion in Imerina) led the Merina court to rely upon *fanompoana* and other non-slave labour (chiefly political prisoners and other convicts) for the standing army and for most industrial and cash crop production – almost all of which was in state control. *Fanompoana* labour was summoned initially by royal request through the heads of districts and villages. This task was facilitated in Imerina by the concentration of the population in the main rice-growing areas, by restrictions upon mobility, and by ideologies of caste and royalty that promoted passivity and acquiescence to hierarchical authority.

In non-Merina regions, recruitment was carried out under the threat of, or with the use of, force. It was accompanied by an ideology of Merina racial superiority, as is reflected in some of their proverbs: '*Adaladala toa Betsileo, ka miarahaba soavaly*' ('To be a simpleton like the Betsileo and salute a horse'); '*Manao toy ny Bezanozano, ka ny vavy indray no feno lovia*' ('To do like the Bezanozano: so it's the women who have a full dish').[4] From 1825–35 and again from 1869, the system of mobilizing *fanompoana* was enhanced by state control of foreign missions, whose schools and churches served in areas under firm Merina control (approximately one-third of the total area of the island) as recruitment centres and whose agents (foreign missionaries and indigenous personnel) oversaw the enrolment of *fanompoana* and in some instances helped allocate and supervise work tasks. A minority of mission school scholars received higher education and subsequently became high-ranking imperial officers. The majority were despatched from school with or without elementary numeracy and literacy into state-controlled industrial workshops (notably in the period *c.*1825–54), into the goldfields (from the early 1880s) and into the imperial army. The army constituted a special case as soldiers, notably from the mid-1850s, were used less for military purposes and increasingly as commercial agents for officers, for whom they peddled imported and locally manufactured goods along the main internal long-distance trade routes.

Protest

The origins (geographic, cultural and ethnic) of forced labour (slave and non-slave) and the way in which it was variously 'recruited', mobilized, allocated work regimes and supervised in large part determined the nature and extent of protest against forced labour.

African slave protest

The nature of slave protest was in large part determined by the ethnic origins and conditions of work of the slaves. Slaves were predominantly of two ethnic origins, continental African (notably Makua) and Malagasy. African slaves comprised both descendants of Africans enslaved generations back (generally termed *Mainty* (literally 'Black'), or *andevon-drazana* ('slaves of the ancestor's)), and *Mosambika* (generally termed *Makoa* on the coast), the generic Merina term for Africans imported in the great slave import surge of the nineteenth century.

In contrast to Malagasy slaves exported to the Mascarenes, there are no recorded instances of attempts by African slaves in Madagascar to sail back to their homeland. This was largely because they had lost all linguistic and other cultural affinities with mainland Africa. In Malagasy terms, they were defined as without ancestors, possessing only masters: '*Raha very kely, manontany razana; fa raha very lehibe, manontany fanompoana*' ('If enslaved when young, they enquire about their ancestors, but if enslaved as adults, they enquire about the work to be done for their masters').[6]

For those African slaves imported during the nineteenth century, reluctance to attempt to regain their homeland may well reflect the lack of a sea-faring tradition, and possibly the fear not only of re-enslavement upon reaching the African littoral or whilst travelling inland, but also of re-assimilation in the increasingly scattered and fractured societies of Nyassa region most subjected to slave raiding. However, it may also stem from relatively good working conditions. African slaves in the Merina Empire constituted valuable property.

Growing impoverishment of free subjects from the 1820s led to a concentration of slave ownership in the hands of court elite and hangers-on. Ordinary subjects were increasingly obliged to relinquish slave ownership altogether, or to become part-owners – an arrangement that generally offered the slave greater choices and better treatment, but that frequently resulted in disputes between part-owners and their inheritors. African slaves of the elite enjoyed mixed fortunes. On the one hand, as people of foreign origin they were believed to possess alien and potent magical powers and thus the group the most subjected to a poison ordeal called *tangena* from which many died. The *tangena* largely disappeared from the mid-nineteenth century in the central regions of the empire, but persisted in remoter areas.[7] The opportunities for slaves to build a stable family life were also restricted by taboos on cross-caste marriage and inability to build up an inheritance as they, their children and their possessions were all considered the property of their master: in the words of two proverbs, *'Toy ny fanahin 'andevo mandevona'*, *Mba ataovy toy ny anana lahy, ka raha maniry, tsongoy'* ('It is the disposition of a slave to waste' 'Treat him as you do herbs; when he grows, pluck him').[8] On the other hand, their working and living conditions were relatively good. African male slaves were chiefly employed as cattle tenders on remote pastures, agricultural labourers, personal attendants or porters, and African female slaves as personal attendants, porters of water and agricultural workers. African male porters comprised a special group. Some 60,000 strong by the 1890s, they monopolized freight and passenger transport and constituted the only large body of wage earners in imperial Madagascar (remitting up to 50 per cent of earnings to their masters at the court) from the 1830s.

There are to date few recorded instances of African slave revolt in Madagascar. A possible contributory factor was the remote and geographically scattered location of some slave settlements. This rendered cooperation and unity difficult. Nevertheless, there existed some pockets of high African slave concentrations where considerable potential existed for building slave cooperation and organization. One was in the main imperial towns (notably Antananarivo, Fianarantsoa, Toamasina and Mahajanga). However, urban slaves and those in the vicinity of the main urban areas – mainly personal attendants and agricultural workers of the Merina elite – sought less to protest against their status as slaves, than to improve the standing of slaves in society. Indeed, it was common, even when a slave had paid his/her master to within a penny of his redemption price, to choose to remain a slave, spending whatever additional income he/she might receive on other items, including the purchase of slaves (*'Toy ny andevo: tompoimanompo'* – 'Like the slave [he has bought]: he [the slave owner] is served while serving'),[9] rather than regain or attain freedom. The reason was that *fanompoana* – unremunerated forced labour for 'free' subjects – was universally regarded as more exploitative than slavery, and they could use any slave they purchased as a substitute for their own labour.

Instead, such slaves sought to improve their lot through acquiring and exploiting key ideological and religious symbols. For example, slaves formed possibly the majority of those who took advantage of Ranavalona I's decision in 1829 to permit her subjects to attend LMS missionary chapels and by extension to establish reading classes. The slaves were attracted by the chapels because the latter accepted the principle of equality amongst believers, whilst the *taratasy* (reading and writing) was traditionally regarded as imbued with supernatural magic power. Conversion to a foreign religion that taught equality threatened the hierarchical caste structure of Malagasy society, while by mastering the *taratasy*, which had traditionally been restricted to a small group often with quasi-sacerdotal office, slaves were acceding to a magic formula that would give them power over most free people. This had revolutionary potential as it envisaged slaves as a group redefining the status of that group through domination of the *taratasy* and participation as equals in a new religion.[10] A few years later, after realizing the threat to the traditional order posed by Christian education and ideology, the crown banned first slave access to Christian chapels and education, and in 1835 closed down the LMS chapels and schools and expelled the missionaries. Although it would appear that slaves maintained a strong presence in the clandestine church from 1835 to 1861, when the Christian missions recommenced their activity in the island in 1862 they took pains that the Merina social hierarchy was reflected within the schools and chapels. This was confirmed by the creation of a state-church in 1869: the court-favoured Protestant missions, headed by the LMS, catered for the Merina elite, forcing the Roman Catholic missionaries to concentrate upon the slave population. Moreover, almost all missionaries accepted slavery in Madagascar, and many benefited from access to court slave labour, or 'redeemed' or purchased slaves whom they subsequently put to work for the missions.[11]

Thus from 1862 the potential of Christianity for changing the status of slaves vanished. Instead, slaves turned to Malagasy ancestral traditions, attempting thereby to redefine the status of African slaves, from being a sub-caste of foreigners, excluded from traditional Malagasy society, to one integral to the system. The occasional usurpation by slave guardians of their master's ancestral tomb in places distant from their owner's residence, or the false claim by freedmen or escaped slaves to an ancestral tomb – as proof of non-*Mainty* status – may be seen in this light. Another example of slave attempts to integrate into the Malagasy belief system is the *ramanenjana*, choreomaniac movements in which royal ancestors were believed to manifest themselves through possessed people – chiefly young female slaves – although it is unclear whether the latter were of continental African or Malagasy origin. Such movements arose at times of crisis – the most famous being the *ramanenjana* of 1862–63 that culminated in attacks upon the newly returned missionaries and helped precipitate the regicide of Radama II.[12]

Another example of concentrated numbers of African slaves is the porterage system that employed up to 60,000 young African males, all of them strong and fit, chiefly on the 200 kilometre route linking Antananarivo and the high plateau (*c.*1,700 metres in altitude) to Toamasina and the east coast.[13] These comprised the *mpilanjana*, the younger and fitter of the two groups of slave porters, who transported passengers at considerable speed over long distances in palanquins, and *mpaka entana*, older but still fit porters who transported freight, generally of 60 kg, split into two bundles balanced on either end of a bamboo pole that rested on their shoulder. They constituted the only group of regular wage earners in imperial Madagascar. Their 'captains' (headman) negotiated wages that included a *vatsy*, or sum for provisions en-route, and conditions of work with hirers (generally foreigners) and were responsible for ensuring the safe arrival of goods and passengers, for arranging for passports for their men and for remitting a percentage of wages to their owners – a cartel formed by the court elite. Under their captains' leadership, the porters formed a strong proto-trade union organization that engaged in a number of tactics, including strikes, in order to obtain better salaries and conditions for their men. Porter wages steadily improved over time, but the porters' occupation remained hazardous and there is no evidence that porters accumulated earnings to ensure a comfortable existence upon retirement, possibly because such earnings would then become the property of the slave owner. Slave porters were renowned for their love of drink and revelry. However, their protests were invariably aimed at employers, rather than at masters and the institution of slavery.

One exception to the relatively passive response of African slaves in imperial Madagascar was the *Mosambika* revolt of the late 1880s. In 1877, Rainilaiarivony, the Merina prime minister and effective dictator, 'liberated' an estimated 150,000 African slaves imported since 1865. This measure, which delighted European governments critical of slavery, and which infuriated slave owners who received no compensation, boosted the labour reserves of the imperial court which channelled the 'emancipated' slaves into forced labour camps. There is little record of mass dissatisfaction by the *Mosambika* until the court started to exploit gold fields from 1883 in an attempt to finance the 1883–85 war against the French, and afterwards to maintain the military build-up against further anticipated French attacks. By the late 1880s, the *Mosambika* employed at the Suberbie and other gold mines in Iboina, in northwest Madagascar, were in revolt, attacking gold mining installations and Merina forts and convoys. There is even evidence that gangs of rebel *Mosambika* took over some gold fields to finance their revolt.

The *Mosambika* revolt is, however, atypical of African slave protest. First, following the 1877 'emancipation', they enjoyed freedmen rather than slave status. This freedom immediately rendered them vulnerable to *fanompoana*. Their revolt must therefore be considered as part of a protest against *fanompoana* and not against slavery. In this context, it is important to note that the Merina regime considered the *Mosambika* rebels to be 'enemies' of the state, that the rebels appealed with success to other 'enemy' elements to join their ranks, and that they remained active even after the French takeover of the island.

Malagasy slave protest

The nature of protest by slaves of Malagasy origin depended largely upon the ethnic origin of the slave. *Zazahova*, or slaves of Merina origin – often enslaved for debt or political offences – rarely protested. First, they were descendants of the imperial 'race' and thus considered themselves apart, and superior to, slaves of non-Merina origin. They sought to retain contact with their families, into whose ranks they aspired to return, and who could redeem their enslaved relative as soon as they had accumulated sufficient capital resources. Protest would lead to further punishment, which could also affect their families. Moreover, flight was difficult: due to Merina imperialism, there existed widespread animosity against the Merina amongst non-Merina, and anyone originating from the imperial heartland risked being killed or enslaved.

By contrast, Malagasy slaves of non-Merina origin held within the empire sought from the time of their enslavement to escape and initially had to be physically restrained: '*Tsy mahafotsy kirobo hamidy gadra, ka very telo-polo*' ('He who won't give a quarter to buy a chain [upon purchasing a new slave] will lose thirty dollars [as the slave will flee]').[14] Hostility to their Merina masters could assume the form of passive non-cooperation: '*Aza manao toy ny andevolahy mahay valiha: asai-manao tsy mety,. nony tsy irahina manao*' ('Don't do like the slave who can play the *valiha* [type of Malagasy guitar]: bidden to play, he won't; and when not bidden, he plays').[15] When grouped together, as were the Tsimanoa, Moromaniry, 'Maroratsy', Antaisoa, 'Maromiasa' and 'Telovohitra' on the crown plantations of the east coast,[16] there was a distinct possibility of revolt as in the 1850s when workers destroyed sugar factories. However, the main form of immediate protest was flight. For most enslaved peoples from the south and west of the island, returning to their home communities was a choice that was normally closed to those slaves whose homelands had been subjected to firm Merina conquest – namely the central plateau and the eastern littoral. Slaves from subjected areas of the empire were forced to flee into the *efitra*, a no-man's land that separated the imperial domain from regions independent of Merina rule. Generally between ten and 40 kilometres wide, its breadth fluctuated over time, and could also include patches of forest and mountainous terrain within the empire. Brigand bands formed in the *efitra*, comprising escaped slaves and felons, political and religious dissidents, and deserters from the imperial army and other forms of *fanompoana*.

Anti-fanompoana protest

As mentioned, many slaves considered slavery preferable to *fanompoana* for the free population – hence the proverb: *'Mpanompon-dRatsimandresy, ka efa nasandratra vao nihareraka'* ('Slaves of Ratsimandresy: when restored to freedom their troubles began').[17] *Fanompoana* was imposed on Merina and non-Merina subjected to the imperial crown. *Fanompoana* assumed two major forms: military and civilian labour – though both shared the same characteristics of being forced and unremunerated labour for the imperial court – although by extension this could take the form of private work (notably construction of houses) for members of the imperial elite.[18]

A major form of *fanompoana* was the army. As in many Muslim countries, the palace guard in Imerina was traditionally drawn from slave ranks – the *Olomainty* and *Tandonaka* royal slaves of respectively African and Merina origin.[19] However, the situation changed with the formation in 1822 of a standing army for the first time. With the huge growth in domestic slavery in the early 1820s, Radama I feared a slave revolt and in consequence ordered his armies in non-Merina regions of Madagascar to kill all males aged ten and over and to enslave only females and children. Initially, only Merina subjects were drafted into the new imperial army, but from at least the Franco-Merina conflict of 1883–85, peoples from the south east of the island also served in the imperial forces, though they formed distinct companies separated from Merina soldiers and were barred from possessing firearms. Mortality in the army was so great until mid-century that some soldiers considered it fortunate to be injured: ' *'Raikitra tery izao!' hoy ilay voa bala tamin' ny feny, 'fa afaka ho borozano aho raha tonga'* ('"Just the very thing!' says the soldier shot in the thigh, 'for I shall be free to be a civilian when I get back')[20] and some would mutilate themselves in an attempt to escape military service. From 1853 to 1880, military service eased as the relentless campaigns against other peoples of the island virtually ceased. However, in the 1880s and early 1890s, military *fanompoana* became more severe as the imperial court prepared to meet the threat from both the French and from Sakalava and Bara war parties.

Subjects summoned on civil *fanompoana* comprised both Merina and non-Merina peoples, who served primarily as industrial, plantation and construction workers. District chiefs were responsible for dividing the population into *fanompoana* units, multiples of which were summoned for large-scale projects. Skilled artisans formed a special case in that they were from the 1820s summoned on full-time *fanompoana*. Unskilled *fanompoana* was generally drafted on a part-time basis, but in response to the needs of the imperial court rather than to those of agricultural production. Exceptions included groups of Antaimoro and Antaifasy forcibly resettled on east coast plantations in the first half of the nineteenth century.[21] Unskilled labour was also drafted on a semi-permanent basis in times of crisis, such as during the Franco-Merina War when women and children as well as men were forced into the goldfields: '*Tahaka ny hadivoanjo ny fanompoana: ka tsy ny momba ny tahony ihany no atao an-karona, fa ny mipetraka amin' ny tany bohazan-tanana koa mba hamenoana ny harona*' ('Doing *fanompoana* is like harvesting earth nuts: not only those on the stem are put into the basket, but also those on the ground that are gathered by hand in order to fill the basket').[22] The result, in both cases, was ultimately disastrous for the imperial economy as artisans abandoned their crafts, small farmers abandoned their fields and agricultural production steadily decreased. Sometimes, workers attacked the symbols of *fanompoana*: the destruction of the Mantasoa industrial complex in the 1850s that ended the Merina 'industrial revolution' was probably a result of worker sabotage: '*Taozavatr' Imantasoa: ny marary manao izay ho vitany; ny finanritra mamono masoandro*' ('The work at Mantasoa: the sick do what they can; the healthy labour until sundown').[23] Of particular importance were the *gadralava*, a penal labour force, first formed by Radama I to construct a stone road between his palace and the former Zoma market in Antananarivo, and who came to include condemned Christians (1836–62) and political dissidents. They were employed full-time in the harshest varieties of industrial work, but often alongside ordinary *fanompoana* labour whom they could not have failed to influence.[24] *Gadralava* were prime candidates for escape, and they were joined in their flight into the *efitra* by increasing numbers of ordinary refugees from *fanompoana*, notably of young unattached males. Those who remained behind grew increasingly fearful and resentful of the court: '*Ny lehibe toy ny vato ambonin 'ny loha, sady mahataho-mahamenatra*' ('The elite are like the stones [carried] on the head [by *fanompoana* labour], they both make afraid and make ashamed').[25]

Political protest: anti-state, anti-imperialist and anti-church

Whilst for most such refugees, flight from 'unfree' labour was the immediate cause of their presence in the *efitra*, once in the *efitra* they turned to brigandry in order to survive: '*Izay manana no anak'andriana, fa izay lany harena jiolaby*' ('He who has riches is a prince, but he who has not is a robber').[26] Thereby, they automatically acquired the status of *fahavalo*, or 'enemy', a status that only served to increase alienation from and antipathy towards the court born of state exploitation and, in the case of the refugee slave, enslavement. Merina political and religious dissidents, many of them fugitive *gadralava*, found such people ready listeners for their more ideologically based opposition to the Merina regime. At the same time, brigand alliances were commonly forged with Sakalava and Bara communities resisting imperial Merina pretensions. In this manner, brigand bands developed an anti-state and anti-imperialist stance.

Brigand bands, and Sakalava and Bara war parties adopted essentially defensive tactics until the 1883–85 Franco-Merina conflict. However, from the mid-1880s, profiting from the imperial regime's preoccupation with the external threat, and from a massive influx into their ranks that resulted from increased *fanompoana*, these bands went on the attack. An increasingly demoralized army proved incapable of containing them, and by the early 1890s they were launching raids into central Imerina. No Robin Hoods, they plundered villagers of their cattle and seized slaves to sell on the west coast. However, the steady flow of ordinary Merina into their ranks indicates some community of interests, and a common enmity to the Merina court.

The crucial test of loyalty to the imperial regime came in 1895 when French troops launched their second major attack on imperial Madagascar. Bad planning and disease bogged French troops down on the coast and they would in all probability have been defeated had the imperial army confronted them. Instead imperial troops deserted en-masse permitting the French to advance with negligible resistance to take Antananarivo. However, when the French declared Madagascar a protectorate under which the existing Merina administration would continue, there was a massive revolt both in the former imperial heartland (the Menalamba) and in lowland regions of the island. Brigand bands formed the core of rebellion in the former where their chief target was not the French, but mission institutions and personnel who had been the primary means of recruitment and supervision of *fanompoana* labour.[27]

Notes

1 J. A. Houlder, *Ohabolana or Malagasy Proverbs* II (Antananarivo: FFMA, 1930), p.3.
2 Gwyn Campbell, 'The Adoption of Autarky in Imperial Madagascar, 1820–1835', *Journal of African History* 28.3 (1987), pp. 395–411.
3 Gwyn Campbell, 'Labour and the Transport Problem in Imperial Madagascar, 1810–1895', *Journal of African History* 21 (1980), pp. 341–56.
4 Houlder, *Ohabolana* II, p. 52.
5 Ibid. p. 46.
6 Ibid. p. 40.
7 Gwyn Campbell, 'The State and Pre-colonial Demographic History: The Case of Nineteenth Century Madagascar', *Journal of African History* 31.3 (1991), pp. 437–9.
8 Houlder, *Ohabolana* II, p. 44.
9 Ibid. p. 41.
10 Gwyn Campbell, 'Crisis of Faith and Colonial Conquest. The Impact of Famine and Disease in late Nineteenth-century Madagascar', *Cahiers d'Études Africaines* 32 (3) 127 (1992), pp. 415–17.
11 Joseph Sewell, *Remarks on Slavery in Madagascar* (London: Elliot Stock, 1876); Gwyn Campbell, 'Missionaries, Fanompoana and the Menalamba Revolt in late nineteenth century Madagascar', *Journal of Southern African Studies* 15.1 (1988), pp. 54–73.
12 Campbell, 'Crisis of Faith'.
13 Campbell, 'Labour and the Transport Problem'.
14 Houlder, *Ohabolana* 11, p. 43.
15 Ibid. p. 42.
16 Fontoynont et Nicol *Les traitants français de la côte est de Madagascar de Ranavalona I a Radama II* (Tananarive, 1940), pp. 11–12, 29–30.

17 Houlder, *Ohabolana* II, p. 45
18 For *fanompoana* see Gwyn Campbell, 'Slavery and Fanompoana: The Structure of Forced Labour in Imerina (Madagascar), 1790–1861', *Journal of African History* 29 (1988) pp. 463–86; idem, 'Missionaries, Fanompoana and the Menalamba Revolt'.
19 Raombana. 'Histoires' (1853), p. 91 – Archives of the Académie Malgache, Tsimbazaza, Antananarivo.
20 Houlder, *Ohabolana* II, p. 39
21 Fontoynont and Nicol *Les traitants.français*, pp. 11–12, 29–30; Campbell, 'Slavery and Fanompoana'.
22 Houlder, *Ohabolana* II, p. 39.
23 Houlder, *Ohabolana* II, p. 39; see also Gwyn Campbell, 'An Industrial Experiment in Pre-colonial Madagascar, 1825–1861', *Journal of Southern African Studies* 17.3 (1991), pp. 525–59.
24 E. Prout, *Madagascar: Its Mission and its Martyrs* (London, 1863), p. 79; Gwyn Campbell, 'The Role of the London Missionary Society in the Rise of the Merina Empire, 1810–1861', PhD thesis, University of Wales (1985), pp. 208–10, 301.
25 Houlder, *Ohabolana* II, p. 40.
26 Ibid. p. 26.
27 Campbell, 'Missionaries, Fanompoana and the Menalamba Revolt'.

6   Forced labour in Madagascar under Vichy, 1940–42

Autarky, forced labour and resistance on the 'Red Island'

Eric Jennings

This chapter explores the recrudescence of forced labour in Madagascar under the ultra-conservative and authoritarian Vichy regime of 1940–42. I will first quickly survey the forms and scope of forced labour in the inter-war years, before analysing how the bleak economic conditions of Madagascar under Vichy, coupled with important ideological shifts by the French government, made for an explosion of forced labour on the island – one that would continue to spiral well after the arrival of the British (May–September 1942) and the Free French (December 1942) administrations on the island. I will also consider forms of resistance and opposition to this increased reliance on forced labour, and assess the place of the years 1940–42 in the larger history of forced labour in Madagascar.

Forms of forced labour and the legacy of the inter-war years

Gillian Feeley-Harnik has pointed out that 'By World War II, the French had enacted more labour laws to govern the economy of Madagascar than existed in almost any other French colony.'[1] Certainly, unfree labour broadly defined was so widespread as to have been inscribed in the very identity of colonial Madagascar. In 1933, the anti-colonial Paris-based newspaper le *Cri des Nègres* dubbed the island '*Madagascar, pays d'esclavage*' ('Madagascar, country of slavery'), referring not to pre-colonial, but to colonial neo-slavery.[2] And throughout the colonial period, as Feeley-Harnik notes again, the French became adept at grafting forced labour onto Malagasy rituals and beliefs. They thereby substituted French authority for the vacuum left after the French conquered Madagascar in 1895, and exiled Queen Ranavalona III to Algeria in 1897. Forced labour, then, was ingeniously crafted by the French themselves as a form of *Asa* or, more often, *fanompoana*.[3] *Fanompoana*, argues Gwyn Campbell, had been a 'form of prestation (requisition) to the crown' which was radically reconfigured and expanded in mid-nineteenth-century Madagascar. At that point, *fanampoana* emerged as a cornerstone for such crucial activities as military recruitment, or Merina colonization. After 1895, the French thus seized this feature of the Malagasy economy and culture, utilizing it to justify coerced labour for everything from public works, to cultivation. Pre-colonial antecedents of French colonial forced labour are thus critical for comprehending the colonial era.[4]

One should be careful to distinguish between varieties of forced labour in colonial Madagascar; though the net result for requisitioned labour was ostensibly the same, penalties under the *Indigénat, prestations* (aka *réquisitions*), or *travaux d'utilité publique* (the indigenous penal code used by the French, requisitions of forced labour, or forced labour on public works) sometimes followed quite different logics. While forced labour under the *Indigénat* code was by definition punitive in its justification, the notorious SMOTIG (Service de la Main d'Oeuvre des Travaux d'Intérêt Général {Division of Labour and Public Works] for its part was rationalized through notions of *mise en valeur* or economic development. The French employed *Prestations* (requisitions), meanwhile, as a substitute for taxation; thus, requisitions tended to reflect, exploit and exacerbate socio-economic disparities. Each of these forms of statute labour saw ebbs and flows in the colonial era. For example, the SMOTIG, established in 1925, was disbanded at the advent of the Popular Front in France in 1936.

The onset of the Second World War, and the autarky engendered by the British blockade of Madagascar between 1940 and 1942, combined with a hardening in colonial ideologies and practices under Vichy, conspired to increase the scope of forced labour in all of its forms on the 'Red Island', precisely after a relative relaxing of forced labour practices in the late 1930s.[5] Timing here is crucial, for Vichy's governors were very much perceived to be turning back the clock to the 1920s. Interestingly the colonial authorities themselves were acutely conscious of operating a reactionary and retrograde return to what they fantasized as a 'feudal' and 'hierarchical' 'natural state' in Madagascar.[6]

Political and structural factors

Although archival gaps render impossible a systematic quantitative analysis of increases in forced labour for the years 1940 to 1942 (with regional files for the east coast of Madagascar still unsorted in the Aix-en-Provence archives), Dox Ratrematsialonina has nonetheless computed that in the regions of Tananarive (Antananarivo), Tamatave (Toamasina), Fianarantsoa, Diego-Suarez, Majunga (Mahajanga) and Morondava alone, 716,604 days of forced labour were served in 1941. In his weighty dissertation, Ratrematsialonina also shows that the number of sentences to forced labour under the *code de l'indigénat* doubled for these same regions between 1939 and 1941.[7]

A host of factors can account for these considerable increases in forced labour between 1939 and 1942. First, in the *longue durée* of Malagasy labour history, the years 1939–42 came on the heels of a relative loosening of forced labour practices under the Popular Front and its abolition of the SMOTIG. Second, the economic hardships of the blockaded island under Vichy rule also account for the administration's recourse to forced labour on such a scale; as I have shown elsewhere, the drive to produce transformed Malagasy schools into veritable ateliers under Vichy.[8] The economic hardship affected everything from rice production to cloth imports; as Lucile Rabearimanana has shown for a region of the central highlands, increased taxation coupled with poor harvests and an almost complete halt in imports of finished goods from overseas made for a substantial drop in the standard of living, especially in rural Madagascar.[9] An increased reliance on forced labour was only one consequence of this grim economic situation: another can be found in the 'Exposition de l'Adaptation Economique' (the Economic Adaptation Fair) held in 1942, which claimed to show how 'Madagascar can continue to get by ... in spite of the isolation resulting from the war'.[10] Thus, the exhibit exhorted local consumers to find substitutes for everything from imported cloths to petrol. Vichy's governors presented forced labour to the Malagasy public in much the same way as they presented ersatz elements: as a belt-tightening measure rendered necessary by the British naval blockade.

Third, the ideological shifts triggered by the island's adherence to Vichy in 1940 played a considerable role in the increase in forced labour. Governors Léon Cayla and Armand Annet clung to Marshal Philippe Pétain's formula of '*Travail, Famille, Patrie*' (Work, Family, Motherland), stressing that the notion of '*Travail*' needed to become anchored in Malagasy culture. In this way, Vichy's local cronies reinvented an oppositional moment – May Day – into a tribute to forced labour.[11] Moreover, the colonial administration in Madagascar, which had once served as a counterweight to outrageous *colon* (white settler) demands for slave labour before 1939,[12] abruptly changed its tune in 1940. This was of course part and parcel of Vichy France's ideological baggage. In Madagascar, hardly surprisingly, unions were suddenly banned, and elaborate plans were drafted to replace them with Mussolini-style corporatist entities. In other instances, metropolitan French laws on the *chantiers de jeunesse*, a group intended to regiment young Frenchmen, were applied to Madagascar's 'unemployed'; here the line between youth outfits and forced labour camps became blurred. But mostly, this shift reflected the ultra-conservative turn of 1940 in France: regional reports from the Vichy era in Madagascar betray hope that the administration's previous 'self-restraint' in meting out forced labour sentences had at last been lifted, thanks to the providential advent of an authoritarian, antirepublican, elitist and hierarchical regime in metropolitan France.[13]

An explosion of forced labour

Regional sources reveal the abruptness with which forced labour was increased starting in July 1940, and the rapid escalation of the practice thereafter. A report from the *chef de district* (district head) Pinon in Mahabo (Morondava region) in 1941 reads: 'Regarding the execution of prestations, an extremely strict control and surveillance has resulted in very strong progress. Over the course of the year 1941, 102,450 days of *prestations* were effectively used, as opposed to only 64,650 days in 1940'.[14] A similar increase was registered by the courts in Majunga: 'the number of penalties meted out under the *indigénat* in 1941 is superior to last year's: 3,385 this year, vs. 2,669 in 1940'.[15] Majunga's *chef de région* (chief of region) added, quite lucidly: 'Requisitions of men have taken on such importance in the region that I must point out that were this form of recruitment to be eliminated after the war, it would need to be phased out gradually over at least six months, or else each and every factory in our region would be forced to close'.[16] In the span of a year, Majunga's industrial output had been so closely tied to forced labour that colonial officials warned of economic chaos were the institution ever to be abolished. Like slavery in the nineteenth-century French sugar colonies, forced labour in Madagascar had become not just an institution, but a system rooted in the fabric of both the colonial society and economy. Interestingly, upon taking control of the island in early 1943, General de Gaulle's Free French representative would essentially concur with this appraisal, deeming forced labour indispensable to pursue the war effort in Madagascar.

'A golden age for *colons*'

Jean Suret-Canale characterized the Vichy era in West Africa in such terms;[17] and much the same could be said of Madagascar. French owners of factories, vanilla estates and graphite mines all revelled in the labour suddenly bountifully provided by the administration. Thus, a certain Bouillon wrote to the head of his district in April 1942:

> I am happy to advise you that the 200 forced labourers currently present at la Mahajamba have given satisfactory results overall. Both in the discipline and regularity of work, there has been considerable progress compared to previous years. It is without a doubt the result of your current hard-line policy, and I am pleased to congratulate the Administration on it.[18]

Certainly, this cheap labour must have translated into handsome profits for colonialist entrepreneurs. Jean-Roland Randiramaro has noted that as more and more labour was requisitioned by force, correspondingly fewer paid labourers were hired. In the northern district of Ambilobe, for example, the number of paid agricultural workers dropped from 955 in 1939 to 579 in 1940.[19]

And yet, not all settlers were content. It would seem that large industrialists, latifundia owners, vanilla magnates and graphite barons reaped most of the profits from Cayla and Annet's penchant for forced labour. In March 1941, a small-time tobacco grower named Buhot de Launay complained from Port-Bergé/Mampikony directly to the governor general:

A few months from now, in April and May, my colleagues and I, tobacco planters, will need vital labour to ensure the clearing of undergrowth and the planting of seedlings. And yet, when we ask the Administration, they respond that there are not enough men; when we insist, they send us a handful of poor devils who haven't paid their taxes. We need a large number of workers at a specific season, not lame labour. This state of affairs is not designed to help small settlers. Could we not choose from the natives who have paid their taxes some who seem to have the privilege of doing nothing all year long ... I hear that the large farms are privileged with respect to labour; too often we forget that it takes many streams to make a big river.[20]

Clearly articulated here are both a new permissiveness concerning forced labour – why not demand *prestations* even from Malagasy who have paid their taxes? – and a sense of resentment that the administration favoured large estates over family farms. Indeed, in July 1942, Governor Annet actually stipulated that only large enterprises or farms, requesting more than 20 workers, would be granted the forced labour they requested.[21]

Naturally, this golden age of forced labour made for excesses of all sorts – even by the standards of the colonial officials advocating and enabling forced labour. For instance, it was brought to the administration's attention that the owner cum principal of the agricultural school of Mazy was shamelessly abusing the *prestation* system. The many dozen requisitioned men who served this man complained bitterly of physical abuse. Of greater concern to the administration, the labourers whom this school principal and part-time entrepreneur claimed to be using to till his vegetable garden were actually being used to rebuild and renovate his home for free. And yet, the administration recommended sending another seven requisitioned labourers to this man, on the grounds that his previous requests for labour 'had been denied, because they came before our current regime of requisitions'.[22] The years 1940–42 thus marked a wholesale shift in the practice of forced labour generally: the administration could now dispense forced labourers for housework in colonial homes, with the knowledge that such an act would have been impossible only a year earlier – indeed to make up for lost time as it were. Under Vichy, the administration felt it needed to compensate for the laxness of previous years. Clearly, then, this era marked a hardening of colonial practices in Madagascar more broadly.

Coercion

A rapid examination of the *Journal Officiel de Madagascar* (the colony's official register of laws and decrees) for this period sheds light on a series of punitive reforms that allowed this remarkable spread of forced labour throughout the whole island. A series of decrees from January 1941 codified how *prestations* were to be imposed, stipulated the rate at which a day's labour would be exchanged for income tax – four francs 50 per day on the Ile de Sainte Marie/Nosy Boraha (the rate hovered between three and five francs per day, depending on the region) – and specified the fines for evading *prestations*. The decree for Sainte Marie also made an interesting exception: 'Those whose social rank did not permit *prestations en nature* (literally payment through personal work) were to be dispensed'.[23] Thus the local elite was spared the rigours of forced labour. Statute labour, although needed, should not threaten the colonial perception of local hierarchies.

Archival sources lend a glimpse of the brashness with which Vichy's governors gave licence to forced labour. Whereas their precursors had often drawn the ire of settlers for withholding labour, Armand Annet dispensed the following instructions in April 1942:

> Although the requisitioning of people has now been exercised for more than two years, some district chiefs still seem unaware that [uncooperative] requisitioned labourers can be punished by more than merely withholding wages or punishments under the *Code de l'Indigénat* [the Indigenous Code]. Indeed, the notice in the *Journal Officiel* of 20 January 1940 ... specifies that requisitioned labourers can be punished ... by six days to five years of prison time for refusing to honour a legal order of requisitioning.[24]

Most administrators had received the message long before. A host of documents reveal that punishments for evading forced labour were frequent indeed in this period. In his November 1941 report, the head of the Fianarantsoa region observed: 'A clear and marked resistance to labour has been noted, especially to *prestations*. As a result, the punishments under the *Code de l'Indigénat* are more frequent than in previous years, when indulgence had bred laziness'.[25] Clearly expressed here was the idea that pre-Vichy (read Popular Front) laxness had now made way to rigour and discipline – notions encapsulated by the recrudescence of forced labour itself.

Forms of resistance

Colonial sources registered constant opposition to the increase of forced labour between 1940 and 1942. As early as June 1940 – a month before the advent of the Vichy regime, at a time when *prestations* were being justified by the war with Germany – Governor de Coppet urged that employers advise the administration of 'irregular absences' of 'requisitioned persons.'[26] He noted that migration of peoples made the task of drawing lists of potential forced labourers increasingly difficult. Here migration, whether deliberately conceived as a strategy to avoid *prestations* or not, had already emerged as a serious spoke in the wheels of the colonial administration in Madagascar.

'Voting with one's feet' was of course one of the easiest ways of avoiding forced labour. This practice was not restricted to the south of the island. In the Befandriana district of the Majunga region an official reported in a July 1942 telegram to his superior that the Sakalava too were practising a form of resistance by migration: 'I have already pointed out in a previous report that the natives do not appreciate in the slightest the recruitment of workers. To escape it, many flee their villages before the arrival of recruiting agents'.[27] The entire Majunga region witnessed widespread opposition to forced labour in this period, as suggested by this October 1941 brief from Soalala: 'I confirm the existence of a general resentment expressed by the native populations towards requisitioning workers for the company known as the 'Marseillais sugar factory' in Namakia'.[28]

So concerned was the administration about the practice of avoiding forced labour by migration that various schemes were suggested to curb this oppositional act. An inspector sent by the governor general to the district of Vangaindrano near Fort-Dauphin (Taolanaro) noted the following local initiative in September 1941:

> Monsieur Lemaitre, who is far from being wrong on this score, complains of the suppression of the *livre barré* (register that kept tabs on workers) which allowed him to follow the movements of workers. 22,693 Antaisakas have left the district between 1930 and 1939, and only 9,445 have returned, the others having settled elsewhere.[29]

Frustrated with nomadic flouting of *prestations*, local officials thus suggested the reintroduction of a booklet designed to enhance surveillance and control of requisitioned peoples.

Epilogue

Finally, when a token of freedom of expression was reintroduced to Madagascar in 1943, mounting hostility to forced labour on the island also exploded through political avenues. In October 1943, the *Amicale des citoyens français d'origine malgache* (Association of French Citizens of Malagasy Origin) – one of the few organizations to represent Malagasy interests at the time, singled out 'forced requisitions of labour . . . as the abuse about which the Malagasy complain the most bitterly'.[30]

The practice of forced labour in Madagascar did not end overnight with the arrival of British forces (primarily East and South African) in Tananarive in September 1942; far from it. In the district of Ambato-Boeni (Majunga region), a report from 1943 noted: 'The system of requisitioning people remains very unpopular. Moreover, it leads to corruption amongst indigenous administrators of all ranks'.[31] In fact, Pierre Boiteau, Roland Randriamaro and Dox Ratrematsialonina have argued that forced labour reached an unmistakable zenith under the Free French representative Legentilhomme in 1943–44, with Madagascar contributing massively to the Allied war effort. Thus in 1943 some 3,810,000 days of forced labour were performed on public works alone.[32] As Frederick Cooper has shown, forced labour would only be theoretically curtailed throughout French colonies in 1946 after much lobbying on the part of Aimé Césaire, Félix Houphouët-Boigny, Léopold Senghor and Lamine Guèye, amongst others.[33]

Notes

1 Gillian Feeley-Harnik, *A Green Estate: Restoring Independence in Madagascar* (Washington: Smithsonian Institution Press, 1991), p. 127.
2 'Madagascar, pays d'esclavage', *Le Cri des Nègres* (July-August 1933), p. 1.
3 Gillian Feeley-Harnik, 'Ritual and Work in Madagascar', in Conrad Kottak, Jean-Aimé Rakotoarisoa, Aidan Southall and Pierre Vérin (eds), *Madagascar: Society and History* (Durham: Carolina Academic Press, 1986), pp. 157–74.
4 Gwyn Campbell 'Slavery and Fanompoana: The Structure of Forced Labour in Imerina (Madagascar), 1790–1861', *Journal of African History* 29:3 (1988), pp. 463–86. Quotation from p. 486.
5 Lucile Rabearimanana refers to an 'accentuation of colonial constraints', to describe the hardening of colonial practices under Vichy – see her 'Résistances et nationalisme', in Evelyne Combeau-Mari and Edmond Maestri (eds), *Le Régime de Vichy dans l'Océan Indien* (Paris: SEDES, 2002), p. 103.
6 Eric Jennings, *Vichy in the Tropics: Pétain's National Revolution in Madagascar, Guadeloupe and Indochina, 1940–1944* (Stanford: Stanford University Press, 2001), ch. 3.
7 Dox F. Ratrematsialonina 'Madagascar pendant la deuxième guerre mondiale. Un essai d'autarcie, 1939–1943,' PhD thesis, Université d'Aix-en-Provence, II, pp. 180, 184–5.
8 Eric Jennings, 'Vichy à Madagascar: la Révolution nationale, l'enseignement et la jeunesse, 1940–1942',*Revue d'histoire moderne et contemporaine* 46.4 (December 1999), pp. 727–44.
9 Lucile Rabearimanana, 'Le district de Manjakandriana (Province d'Antananarivo) pendant la deuxième guerre mondiale: désorganisation économique et restructuration sociale', *Omaly Sy Anio* 29–32 (1989–90), pp. 433–55.
10 Archives Nationales, Centre des Archives d'Outre-mer, Aix-en-Provence (hereafter CAOM), Madagascar PM 121.
11 Jennings, *Vichy in the Tropics*, pp. 205–7.
12 As Jennifer Cole has noted, French colonial settlers complained already in 1901 that corvées were not coercive enough. Jennifer Cole, *Forget Colonialism? Sacrifice and the Art of Memory in Madagascar* (Berkeley: University of California Press, 2001), p. 53.
13 Jennings, *Vichy in the Tropics*, pp. 60–61,
14 CAOM, Madagascar 2D 126, Rapport annuel 1941.
15 CAOM, Madagascar 2D 136, Rapport annuel 1941.
16 Ibid.
17 Jean Suret-Canale, *Afrique noire* (Paris: Editions Sociales, 1964) II, p. 578.
18 CAOM, Madagascar, 6 (2) D 20.
19 Jean-Roland Randriamaro, *PADESM et luttes politiques à Madagascar* (Paris: Karthala, 1997), p. 44. Lucile Rabearimanana has likewise remarked on the handsome profits for *colons* during this era. Rabearimanana, 'Résistances et nationalisme', p. 113.
20 CAOM, Madagascar 3B 512, Buhot de Launay au Gouverneur Général.
21 CAOM, Madagascar 3A 27, 'Circulaire 47 IT'.
22 On the École/ferme du Mazy, see CAOM, Madagascar, PT 145, 'Main d'oeuvre'.

23 *Journal Officiel de Madagascar* (25 January 1941), p. 83.
24 CAOM, Madagascar 3A 27, Circulaire 29 IT, 3 April 1942.
25 CAOM, 3B 534, 'Région de Fianarantsoa, état d'esprit de la population'.
26 CAOM, Madagascar 3A 15 (2), 19 June 1940.
27 CAOM, Madagascar PM 124, rapport 1941: Telegram from Befandriana to Majunga, 29 July 1942.
28 Ibid. Soalala to Majunga, 1 October 1941.
29 CAOM, Madagascar 3D 331, inspection des 9 et 10 septembre 1941, p. 19.
30 Archives Nationales de Madagascar, D 697, 'Revendications de l'Amicale des citoyens français d'origine malgache,' petition (6 October 1943).
31 CAOM, Madagascar 2D 3 (3), Ambato-Boéni, Rapport annuel 1943.
32 Pierre Boiteau, *Contribution à l'histoire de la nation malgache* (Paris: Editions sociales, 1958), p. 256.
33 Frederick Cooper, *Decolonization and African Society: the Labour Question in French and British Africa* (Cambridge: Cambridge University Press, 1996), pp. 187–9.

7 Sugar and servility

Themes of forced labour, resistance and accommodation in mid-nineteenth-century Java

*G. Roger Knight**

Introduction

The case of colonial-era sugar production on the Indonesian island of Java is important to any global re-assessment of themes related to worker subordination and resistance in the context of servile or unfree labour. On the basis of industrialized manufacture unparalleled elsewhere in Asia, the Java sugar industry entered the ranks of major producers for a rapidly growing international trade in the commodity during the middle decades of the nineteenth century. Indeed, from about 1870 onward, Java stood second only to Cuba as an exporter of cane sugar to world markets. Java's colonial sugar industry, however, has tended to be considered *sui generis* and isolated from discussions of New World sugar production because of Java's geographic location and the predominantly insular character of its own extensive historiography.

This degree of neglect is all the more regrettable in that it disguises the fact that after the mid-nineteenth century the world's two largest producers of industrially manufactured cane sugar, Java and Cuba, depended upon systems of servile labour. The fact that one was designated as practising slavery and the other forced labour of peasants should not detract from the need to place the experience of servile labour on Java in a global perspective that establishes its relevance to ongoing New World debates. Nor should it lead to the supposition that 'plantation slavery' constituted a labour process so unique and homogeneous as to invalidate comparison across continents of either the modes of subordinating labour, or of the modes of resistance to that subordination. In short, nineteenth-century Java, in tandem with other regions of Asia, belongs as much to the debate about unfree labour and resistance as do Cuba and other parts of the New World.

In the case of nineteenth-century Java, as with the New World, received notions of a homogeneous and transhistorical form of servile labour have been eroded by recent scholarship which has made clear just how heterogeneous, multi-faceted and evolving the forms of servility actually were.[1] The traditional, constrictive free vs. forced labour dichotomy merely skims over the surface of issues of rural political economy, providing little more than a rudimentary, even simplistic answer to the question of how workers are mobilized and controlled. Modern scholarship on Java, much like its New World counterpart, has highlighted significant groups of workers, alongside the conventionally servile labour, who were neither free nor servile in the strictest sense.

All this is apparent, though not always explicit, in the existing literature. What is a good deal less apparent, however, are the implications of this revised view of servile labour for our understanding of the forms of resistance and *accommodation* which servility engendered. In the light of this, the purpose of this chapter is twofold. The first is to outline the main findings of recent scholarship with respect to servile labour in the mid-nineteenth-century Java sugar industry. The second is to relate these findings to the issue of resistance, which was as multi-layered and ambiguous in Java as its counterparts in the Caribbean and the Americas.[2]

The *Cultuurstelsel*, servile labour and the produciton of sugar in nineteenth-century Java

The focus of the chapter is the *Cultuurstelsel* or government-imposed System of Cultivations that provided the basis for sugar production in colonial Java for more than half a century between the 1830s and the 1880s. Java – the most populous and fertile island of the Indonesian archipelago – was the site of a sugar industry that had been first established in the course of the seventeenth century under the aegis of the Dutch East India Company (VOC), which came to control most of the coastal districts of the island until its bankruptcy and takeover by the Dutch state at the end of the eighteenth century. By the early 1800s, the colonial sugar industry on Java had become largely moribund. The *Cultuurstelsel* revived and greatly expanded it as part of a larger, state-run project to harness the island's agricultural resources for the large-scale production of commodities for the world market. Nonetheless, the Java sugar complex differed substantially from most of its New World counterparts, in so far as it was located within a much larger socio-economy of rice-growing peasants and the indigenous, Javanese elites who dominated them.

The *Cultuurstelsel* arose in the wake of the Java War of 1825–30, a struggle for power in Central Java between the Dutch (and their local allies) and their Islam-inspired opponents under the Javanese *pangeran* (Prince) Dipanegara. Its conclusion saw the Dutch confirmed in their position as Java's unchallenged colonial rulers and ready, under Governor-General Van den Bosch, to reorganize several key sectors of commodity production, sugar included. Under the aegis of the *Cultuurstelsel*, reorganization was predicated on the compulsory cultivation of export staples by the Javanese peasantry, recruited and supervised by Dutch and Javanese state officials and their own village headmen or *lurah*. Sugar cane produced in this fashion in Java during the mid-nineteenth century decades was subsequently processed into sugar in a network of largely Dutch-run factories that likewise relied heavily on forced labour for their successful operation.

The issue of forced labour in the Java sugar industry under the aegis of the *Cultuurstelsel* excited considerable comment in contemporary colonial circles. During the 1850s and 1860s, both in The Netherlands and Java itself, there took place an extended debate among colonial officials, sugar manufacturers and capitalists about the servile nature of the workforce associated with the *Cultuurstelsel* and the potential in Java for the evolution of free labour. This gave rise to an often-fierce polemic which served to confirm the *Cultuurstelsel*'s reputation as forced labour regime.[3] Nonetheless, existing and ongoing research suggests that as an instance of servile labour it was a regime of a highly particular and remarkably complex kind.[4]

We can start by disposing of any idea that forced labour was predicated exclusively or – in some parts of Java at least – even predominantly on the need to extract labour forcibly from an essentially homogeneous peasantry that was largely self-sufficient. In fact, labour was (notionally) available to the sugar industry from a pool of landless households, as well as from the landholding peasants who comprised the greater part of the rural working population. The point was that many of the lowland areas of rural Java were characterized in the mid-nineteenth century decades by a significantly skewed access to resources among a peasantry that knew of a significant economic divide between landholders and those households that could be counted as actually or functionally landless. As such, they were dependents (*menumpang*) of the landed, among whom there was also an appreciable differentiation in terms of access to land and possession of livestock resources in the form of water buffalo used for ploughing. In short, Java's mid-nineteenth-century peasantry was one in which the existence of 'haves' and 'have-nots' was sufficiently in evidence for it to form an important element in the industry's mobilization of labour.

Under the aegis of the *Cultuurstelsel*, forced labour was mobilized by the colonial authorities in the form of an obligation laid on the peasantry to perform labour service or *corvée*. Colonial sources designated such labour, in appropriately feudal terminology, as *Heeredienst* or *Cultuurdienst* – lord-service or cultivation-service. Though the situation varied considerably over time, and from one part of Java to another, the degree of differentiation among the peasantry was strongly reflected in the way in which obligations to perform labour service were actually met. Some landholders met some of their obligations directly from within their own households: that is to say, they worked the cane fields and participated in harvest work themselves, in conjunction with members of their immediate family. What was also widely reported, however, was that landholders supplied substitutes for at least some of the tasks they were called upon to perform, and that these substitutes were drawn from their own dependent *menumpang* or else – for a payment in cash or kind – from the general pool of village landless (who might be *menumpang* or possibly *bujang* – landless, young and unmarried males).

The complexities of servile labour in mid-nineteenth-century Java were compounded, moreover, by the fact that although labour might be compulsory, it was not unpaid. Peasant landholders assigned to work in preparing and planting cane fields were remunerated with a crop-payment (*plantloon*) paid by state officials, while those drafted into harvest work received a kind of dole from the factories that was fixed by the state. Landholders who sent substitutes to perform harvest work, and many of them did, had to supplement this dole with an additional payment. The distribution of crop-payments is uncertain. Given the asymmetrical nature of the relations of production prevailing among the landholding element in the villages, it would be naïve to assume that it was evenly spread. Nonetheless, some elements among the peasantry can be presumed to have benefited significantly or even substantially. Within an overall framework of servile labour, there were clearly winners as well as losers.

Though servile labour of the kind designated as *Heeredient* or *Cultuurdienst* predominated, some categories of work performed in the industry did not fall under this rubric. By the 1850s, at least, not all cane cutters were 'Government Coolies' – as they were described in contemporary usage – drafted into fieldwork on the basis of *Heeredienst*. Some harvest workers were what colonial sources referred to as *vrijwilligers* (literally volunteers). These were recruited in the adjacent villages or further afield by *mandur* (foremen or gangers) who were supplied by the factory with the money necessary to make cash advances to labourers that bound them to appear for work. Such bonding remained informal, however, in the sense that, despite the best efforts of the industry, the Indies Government never created penal sanctions for the breaking of labour contracts, such as applied in much of the Outer Islands of The Netherlands Indies by the late nineteenth century.

A further and varying proportion of the industry's workforce was drawn from the ranks of what the factory managements described as vagabonds, itinerant workers who moved around the countryside taking a wage (or possibly somebody's chicken or a small cloth full of sugar) wherever they could find it. Within the factories themselves, there were groups of workers, generally the more skilled, who were informally bonded rather than servile in the manner just described, and who were paid by the owners on a regular, sometimes all-year-round basis. At many factories the cane carters, the people who brought in cane from the fields on buffalo-hauled *pedati* (two-wheeled, 'native' carts), formed a quite distinct category of labour. Their work was crucial because cane needed to be processed as quickly as possible after cutting before its sucrose content began to convert into invert sugars (fructose, glucose) that were impossible to crystallize. In many parts of Java by the 1850s, haulers had formal contracts with the factories, and were in receipt of a quite substantial cash advance. In this sense they constituted a form of bonded – and hence possibly of servile – labour. Their possession of carts and buffaloes, however, placed them in a category of considerable economic substance in a countryside characterized by small peasant holdings of land and livestock. At many mid-century factories, haulers had contracts based on cash advances that they received prior to the start of the manufacturing season, advances which they used to buy or build carts, hire or buy water-buffalo or oxen to pull them and as a means to advance cash to their own teams of workers.

In short, under the rubric of 'forced labour', the large-scale commodity production of sugar in mid-nineteenth-century Java was associated with a variety of labour processes, in most of which 'simple' coercion was only one of the defining elements. The commandeering of labour under the aegis of the *Cultuurstelsel* undoubtedly involved many physical brutalities and constraints of a more-or-less systematic character. It was not until some time in the 1860s, for example, that corporal punishment was formally restricted as a means of ensuring obedience. Yet coercion needs to be contextualized if it is to be understood, and – as in the case of the New World – the mobilization and disciplining of labour is more productively viewed as a complex continuum of processes rather than in terms of the classic polarities of servile or free.

Resistance and revolt

The history of resistance and revolt in the context of forced sugar product in mid-nineteenth-century Java is one in which what did *not* happen is as important as what did. The classic peasant revolts of nineteenth-century Java – integral to the so-called Java War of 1825–30 and recurrent notably in the far west of the island at the end of the 1840s and again at the end of the 1880s – occurred either prior to the imposition of the forced labour regime in sugar production or else in areas where it was never introduced. On present evidence, one of the very few violent insurrections in the mid-nineteenth century that had an unequivocal connection to the sugar industry and its servile workforce took place in the Central Java Residency of Tegal in the mid-1860s. Some 70 men attacked a military barracks in the town of Tegal, as well as the house of the *Regent* or *Bupati* of Tegal (the leading Javanese official in the area) and a sugar factory on the outskirts of the town. They then headed into the major sugar producing region to its immediate south before being rounded up by the Regent's own native troops and as many as a hundred colonial troops sent from the city of Semarang, more than a hundred kilometres away. The damage to industry installations was not substantial and the rebels appear to have killed only one man, the Javanese clerk of the town's *Jaksa* (a legal official), but their progress through the countryside had the effect of causing the European personnel at most of the region's factories to flee to the safety of Tegal town.[5]

There were certainly protests, especially during the earlier stages of the implementation of the *Cultuurstelsel*, when fairly numerous peasant reactions were recorded against the imposition of new and increased forms of servitude. In one notable instance, in the north coast town of Pekalongan in

October 1842, some 600 sugar-planting peasants assembled in front of the house of the Dutch Resident, protesting against the inadequate remuneration which they had been accorded for their compulsory work in the cane fields. Prevailed upon by the Javanese Regent and his Head *Jaksa* to return to their homes, they nonetheless came back the following morning, when it was only 'with great difficulty' that the Regent again persuaded them to disperse. However, the colonial record on the subject does not imply that there was anything menacing about the 'incident' or that the threat of violence hung in the air – something which appears to be confirmed by the mild reprisals subsequently visited on the ostensible organizers of the demonstration.[6] Elsewhere, in East Java in the 1830s, demonstrations of this kind took on a potentially more violent form.[7] Even so, such protest was profoundly localized, sporadic, apparently spontaneous and of short duration.

If concerted, violent resistance was rare, so too was cane burning on any appreciable, recorded scale. It was certainly prevalent in the late nineteenth century, and at times in the early twentieth reached endemic proportions. In the mid-nineteenth-century decades, however, it was largely absent. Moreover, despite its reputation as the classic form of protest against the sugar industry, cane burning actually constitutes a deeply problematic form of 'resistance'. On examination, it might turn out to have at least as much to do with animosities among the workforce and among landholders themselves as it had with resistance toward the sugar industry per se.[8]

Other forms of resistance to the imposition of servile labour were recurrent, however, and had obvious parallels with resistance to slavery in the Caribbean and elsewhere in the New World. The flight of peasants away from sugar-growing districts was widely reported in the first two decades of *Cultuurstelsel* production (1830–50),[9] and may well have had its corollary in the communities of 'vagabonds' (see above), who might yet be drawn into the orbit of sugar production on a temporary basis in return for wages. One leading scholar has referred to them as 'living in the twilight zone between *bujang* and bandit'.[10] Probably the great majority of peasants who sought some escape from servitude did so by resettling in the expanding nineteenth-century frontier of wet-rice agriculture in parts of the east-central Java (notably the upper Brantas valley) where sugar had yet to reach. Nonetheless, flight took place in a broader context in which the mobility of the rural population of the Java lowlands had long been commented upon.[11] As we shall see, however, that mobility appears to have been curbed significantly by mid-century developments. As Elson remarks, 'the great majority of peasants neither rebelled nor fled but stayed where they were and tried to make the best of their changed situation'.[12] This did not preclude, of course, a certain dragging of peasant feet that almost certainly constituted the most prevalent form of servile labour's resistance to the inroads of the sugar industry in the mid-century decades. Manifested as what irate colonial manufacturers saw in terms of 'poor cultivation' and 'inadequate attention' and 'insufficient turn out of labour', this might result in exemplary punishment for those supervisors, usually village headmen and their underlings, to whom this neglect of duty could be sheeted home. Sometimes, members of the Javanese *priyayi* elite might be disciplined for allowing such things to happen. This remained, however, at most a muted form of resistance and as the *Cultuurstelsel* matured became largely exceptional in its incidence.

Indeed, the most effective forms of resistance to the industry may well have come from elements among the industry's workforce who were among the least servile: the haulers of factory cane, people who, as we have already observed, were debt-bonded to the industry, but who operated outside the servitude of *Cultuurdienst* and *Heeredienst* that characterized the bulk of the mid-century workforce. At some factories, at least, it is quite apparent that the haulers were well aware of the strong position that they had by virtue of their key position in the production process as the crucial link between field and factory. Indeed, so inclined were they to cause 'trouble' in respect to remuneration and conditions that at one factory the owners installed a tramway precisely to reduce their dependency on haulers. The situation is one that points to the problematic nature of the dichotomy between resistance *and* accommodation. In this case, far from being polar opposites, they were two sides of the same coin: for the haulers to resist the factory, they first had to have entered into an accommodation with it.[13]

The political economy of servitude

As we have just seen, by most accepted measures, resistance to the servitude imposed by the sugar industry, though not absent from mid-nineteenth century Java, was not present to the degree that might be assumed, given the burdens imposed on the peasantry by the expansion of the production of sugar in the colony between the 1830s and the 1860s and its implications for those workers who were coerced into its labour force in both field and factory. Some Dutch contemporaries were not adverse to cultural explanations of the phenomenon, and on occasion were apt to cite the reputed 'docility' of the Javanese and their 'slavish' subordination to their 'chiefs'.[14] The present argument, however, draws attention to two aspects of the political economy of rural Java in the mid-nineteenth-century that may offer a more convincing explanation. The first point to be made is that the system of accommodation as well as coercion that underpinned Dutch power in nineteenth century Java prevented the industry from pushing its demands on servile labour to the extremes that might have engendered endemic resistance. The second point concerns the colonial transformation of Java's peasantry and its implications for resistance and accommodation.

The starting point for discussion of the political economy of servitude in mid-nineteenth-century Java is the fact that the sugar industry's demands for labour represented only part of a wider servitude within which the peasantry was enmeshed. In reporting to his employers on his difficulties in obtaining workers other than forced labour, one very prominent mid-century factory manager remarked that:

> there is not a single peasant who is not subject to the orders of half a dozen functionaries. That may not be written in the Statute Book, but it is written in the book of facts. Not one of the dwellers in the *desa* [villages] who has a household and status has the free disposal of his own time, and he cannot sell that to me which he himself is unable to dispose of.[15]

Within this context, the colonial political economy in which the sugar industry was located was, of necessity, heavily dependent on accommodation between Dutch colonialists, indigenous, *priyayi* elites (the 'functionaries' just mentioned) and the peasant villagers. The colonial presence, both civil and military, was numerically tiny, even by the prevailing standards of European colonial hegemony. Such might as the Indies Government possessed was deployed first and foremost in expeditions in the Outer Islands of an insular empire that was far from fully consolidated in the mid-century decades. In Java itself, the 'strong arm' of colonial power had, of necessity, to be tempered by the 'blind eye' of compromise with, and accommodation to, local interests. This tempered, very significantly, both the reach of the system of forced labour associated with the *Cultuurstelsel* and its potential repercussions in terms of resistance and revolt.

The pervasive nature of the 'blind eye' of compromise and accommodation in rural Java in the mid-century decades with respect to the deployment of manpower resources in particular emerged very clearly in the 1860s, when the Dutch finally began to assert themselves to achieve something approximating to an accurate (or at least greatly improved) head count. In one, unexceptional part of the heavily 'sugared' north coast of the island, it was 'discovered' that around 20 per cent or more of the available manpower had been concealed, apparently for decades, from prying colonial eyes.

The reason we know about this significant underestimation of the population in the area is because of the work of the Indies Government's Statistical Survey (*Statistiek Opname*), a joint civilian-military enterprise conducted by a team specifically appointed and trained for the purpose by the Indies Government. The work of the Survey represented a significant departure from the deference to native informants which had hitherto characterized attempts at enumeration in the countryside. These relied on information supplied to the *controleurs* and Residents by *wedana* and *bupati*. In one well-documented instance, it was reported that the enumeration was carried out by the 'eldest legitimate son' of the Regent, and that there was no doubt that the result was well below the actual population of the area concerned. The reporting officer conceded that a more accurate result would be obtained if a European official conducted a head count from house to house, but that such a procedure would cause a lot of upset ('de bevolking ...

verwekken'). Moreover, just in case the implication of this was not crystal clear, the reporting officer added that he would only alter the arrangement if he were specifically ordered to do so by the Indies Government.[16] The Survey, on the other hand, carried out its own direct inquiries. The results are on first viewing surprising, but on deeper consideration of the method of the previous censuses highly predictable. In the district already alluded to (Pekadjangan, in Pekalongan Residency, Central Java) the population was said to be 18.75 per cent more numerous in 1869 than recorded two years earlier. Equally significant, however, is the history of 'recorded' population growth in Pekadjangan from 1857 to 1867. Comparison between the data available for the two dates suggests the population of Pekadjangan was 68 per cent greater in 1867 than it had been a decade earlier. Even allowing for some degree of immigration into the district, this would suggest the demographically highly improbable sustained rate of increase of around 6 per cent a year. In short, it must be concluded that in the mid-1850s Dutch officials took a much more 'relaxed' attitude to enumeration than did their successors a decade or so later. The earlier 'relaxed' approach did a great deal to 'lubricate' the system of servile labour put into place under the aegis of the *Cultuurstelsel*.[17] In short, servility was 'domesticated' to a degree that can hardly have failed to have an impact on resistance.

But there was more at stake than simply the domestication of servility. The mode of evolution of servile labour also impacted very considerably on peasant responses. The *Cultuurstelsel* sought to locate its demands for labour within an existing framework of labour service that the nineteenth-century Indies Government had inherited from the pre-colonial state in Java. In fact, it almost certainly increased demands on labour substantially, as well as making them more regular (and made a direct call on land through its requisition for cane that had little to do with earlier relations of production between peasants and the elites). Nonetheless, the demand for labour on the part of the state and its officials was something to which generations of peasants had been habituated long before the *Cultuurstelsel* and its associated sugar industry came into existence. Of course, habituation did not necessarily imply that peasant resistance to servitude prior to the 1830s and the implementation of the *Stelsel* had been non-existent. On the other hand, it does serve to temper any implication that servitude was sufficiently novel to have triggered resistance.

This factor of continuity lies close to the heart of other explanations of the 'muted' resistance to the imposition of servile labour associated with the *Cultuurstelsel* and its attendant sugar industry. These explanations stress the 'resilience' of Java's 'long-standing' peasantry in the face of new demands on both labour and land. Robert Van Niel, a leading figure in research on the period, contends that 'local arrangements eventually made by the peasants [prevented] ... the collapse of Javanese housekeeping arrangements.... These *adjustments* and others made the System bearable'.[18] R. E. Elson, whose *Village Java under the Cultuurstelsel* stands as the single most authoritative work on the era, comes at the problem from a different angle but arrives at an appreciably similar conclusion. A careful examination of the colonial historical record inclines him to argue that the *Cultuurstelsel*'s demand on land and labour were not irreconcilable with the requirements of peasant subsistence. By and large, people continued to be able to support themselves from the fields at their disposal. In broad terms, food production per capita was not adversely affected by the call on resources imposed by the *Cultuurstelsel*. Indeed, on balance, the *Stelsel* brought a modest prosperity. The great mass of the rural population continued to live as *peasants* in the sense that they either worked their own plots of land or had reasonably assured access to the land of others as share-croppers, tenants or live-in labourers.

Continuity remains debatable, however, the more so if we accept that terms such as peasant and peasantry are themselves historically highly problematic. Indeed, an alternative (or, at least, complementary) reading of the situation in rural Java in the mid-nineteenth century might posit that resistance and accommodation to servile labour can only be fully understood in the context of an ongoing 'peasantization' of elements of the workforce.[19] It has long been understood, of course, that the expansion of large-scale commodity production in nineteenth-century Java did not proceed in tandem with expropriation of the landed peasantry. In the case of sugar, the issue of expropriation was side-stepped by a system of annual field-exchange that enabled cane to be fitted into the existing agricultural cycle. An elaborate system of crop-rotation saw sugar cane alternating with rice and other crops in a manner which left the fundamentals of peasant agriculture notionally undisturbed. What has been less frequently observed is the extent to which sugar cane and the mid-nineteenth-century Javanese peasantry not only found but also *made* each other. Elements within Java's rural population became more 'peasant-like' in the mid-century decades, in the sense of being less mobile,[20] more unambiguously tied to village communities, more decisively bound into an agrarian economy. This peasantization was by no means the inevitable result of the *Cultuurstelsel*. Indeed, in the early phases of its history in relation to sugar, the officials in charge of the *Stelsel* sought to mobilize labour in some parts of Java through a crude 'en masse' recruitment of workers that had very different implications. By the mid-century, however, the levying of labour had taken an altogether more settled, routine form, and the cultivation of cane had taken on the dimension of what one leading colonial official described as a '*bevolkingscultuur*' (literally people's cultivation), carried out at the usual tempo of 'village' agriculture. This may, of course, have an unduly benign and self-serving view, but it does underline that dimension of servile labour that placed it firmly within the orbit of mundane, 'peasant' production.

The potential ramifications of these developments were considerable, not least that which fused servile labour with peasantization. On the one hand, it reinforced a settled order in the countryside while on the other it created a situation in which authority was very diffuse. Far from promoting a rootless rural society, dominated by serf-labourers with little or no access to land, it both perpetuated and added strength to an element in the village communities that had an interest, however tenuous, in stability. The dynamics of the enmeshment of the rural population in the operations of the sugar industry were so convoluted as to have major implications for resistance, which in consequence was likely to have lacked any readily identifiable focus.

Conclusion

Mid-nineteenth century Java had a sugar industry as heavily based on servile labour as that of Cuba, its New World coeval. In Java's case, however, it was locally domiciled peasants who were pressed into service rather than African slaves. The issue of resistance and revolt in Java among the many thousands of peasants coerced into work in the colony's sugar fields and factories has to be seen in the context of a political economy of servitude which embraced virtually the entire working population of the island. Resistance took a multiplicity of forms, but violent revolt was highly exceptional and the most common form of protest amounted to a dragging of peasant feet in matters of labour turn out, attention to cane cultivation and such like. Over time, resistance appears largely to have atrophied.

The history of resistance among the servile workers of nineteenth-century Java is arguably best understood, however, by reference to two aspects of the political economy of servitude. One is that forced labour in sugar was enmeshed within a system of coercion *and* accommodation that significantly limited the likelihood that the pressure on servile labour would be such as to ferment resistance and revolt. The second is that the colonial transformation of the Javanese peasantry during the mid-century decades, in tandem with the very diffuse nature of servitude itself, acted to inhibit peasant resistance. Together, these factors go some way toward accounting for a degree of acquiescence in servitude that might otherwise seem inexplicable.

Notes

* Associate Professor Knight acknowledges the financial support of the University of Adelaide Special Studies Scheme in researching and writing this chapter.
1 Major studies of the industry and its workforce include Peter Boomgaard, *Children of the Colonial State. Population Growth and Economic Development in Java 1795–1880* (Amsterdam: Free University Press, 1989); Peter Boomgaard, 'Why Work for Wages. Free Labour in Java 1600–1900', *Economic and Social History in the Netherlands* 2 (1991), pp. 37–56; Jan Breman, *Control of Land and Labour in Colonial Java* (Dordrecht: Foris Publications, 1983); R. E. Elson, *Javanese Peasants and the Colonial Sugar Industry: Impact and Change in an East Java Residency, 1830–1940* (Singapore: Oxford University Press, 1984), R. E. Elson, *Village Java under the Cultuurstelsel* (Sydney: Allen & Unwin, 1994); Cees Fasseur, *The Politics of Colonial Exploitation*, translated and edited by R. E. Elson and Ary Kraal (Ithaca NY: Southeast Asia Program, Cornell University, 1992); M. R.

Fernando, 1982, 'Peasants and Plantation: The Social Impact of the European Plantation Economy in Cirebon Residency from the *Cultuurstelsel* to the End of the First Decade of the Twentieth Century', PhD. thesis, Monash University, 1982; G. Roger Knight, *Colonial Production in Provincial Java: the Sugar Industry in Pekalongan-Tegal, 1800–1942* (Amsterdam: V.U. Press, 1993); Djoko Suryo, 'Social and Economic Life in Rural Semarang under Colonial Rule in the Later Nineteenth Century', PhD. thesis, Monash University, 1982; Robert Van Niel, *Java under the Cultivation System* (Leiden: KITLV Press, 1992).

2 See for example the discussion in Laird W. Bergad, *Cuban Rural Society in the Nineteenth Century* (Princeton: Princeton University Press, 1990), pp. 80–5 and 229–59. See in addition, Rebecca J. Scott, *Slave Emancipation in Cuba: The Transition to Free Labour, 1860–1899* (Princeton, NJ: Princeton University Press, 1984), 'Labour Control in Cuba after Emancipation', in Malcolm Cross and Gad Heuman (eds), *Labour in the Caribbean. From Emancipation to Independence* (London: MacMillan, 1987), pp. 80–9; Mary Turner, 'Chattel Slaves into Wage Slaves: A Jamaican Case Study', in Cross and Heuman, *Labour in the Caribbean*, pp. 14–31; Stanley L. Engerman, 'Contract Labour, Sugar and Technology in the Nineteenth Century Caribbean', *Journal of Economic History* 43. 3 (1983), pp. 635–59; Dale W. Tomich, *Slavery in the Circuit of Sugar* (Baltimore: Johns Hopkins University Press, 1990).

3 Fasseur, *Colonial Exploitation*, pp. 162–184.

4 For a discussion of the issues raised in this and the following paragraphs, see G. Roger Knight 'Peasant Labour and Capitalist Production in Late Colonial Indonesia: The Campaign at a North Java Sugar Factory 1840–1870', *Journal of Southeast Asian Studies* 19. 2 (1988), pp. 245–65, 'The Peasantry and the Cultivation of Cane in Nineteenth Century Java', in A. Booth, W. J. O'Malley and Anna Weidemann (eds), *Indonesian Economic History in the Dutch Colonial Era* (New Haven: Yale University Southeast Asian Series, 1990), pp. 49–66; R. E. Elson, 'Sugar Factory Workers and the Emergence of 'Free Labour' in Nineteenth Century Java', *Modern Asian Studies* 20 (1) (1986), pp. 139–74, 'The Mobilisation and Control of Peasant Labour in Java in the Early Cultuurstelsel', in R. J. May and W. J. O'Malley (eds), *Observing Change in Asia* (Bathurst NSW: Crawford House, 1989), pp. 73–93.

5 Tine Ruiter, 'The Tegal Revolt of 1864', in D. Kooiman *et al.* (eds), *Conversion, Competition and Conflict. Essays on the Role of Region in Asia* (Amsterdam: Free University Press, 1984).

6 The four 'ringleaders' were removed for a year to a labour camp. See S. van Deventer, *Bijdragen tot de kennis van het Landelijk Stelsel op Java* (Zalt-Bommel: Joh. Noman), 3 vols 1865–66, vol. 3, pp. 176–80.

7 Elson, *Javanese Peasants*, pp. 54–60.

8 Virtually the only modern discussion of cane burning (dealing primarily with its twentieth-century manifestations) is R. E. Elson, 'Cane Burning in the Pasuruan Area: An Expression of Social Discontent', in F. van Anrooij *et al.*, *Between People and Statistics* (The Hague: Martinus Nijhoff, 1979), pp. 219–34.

9 For specific instances on Java's north coast in the 1840s, see Indies Besluiten 23.5.1846/3 and 9.4.1849/9, Archief Nationaal (hereafter AN), The Hague, Archief Kolonien 2682 and 2717. The issue of flight is widely commented upon, however, in virtually all the historical literature already cited.

10 Boomgaard, *Colonial State*, p. 27.

11 Elson, *Village Java*, pp. 10–13.

12 Elson, *Javanese Peasants*, p. 160.

13 The documentation is in the correspondence (and attachments) from the Batavia Branch Office of The Netherlands Trading Company (NHM), owners of the factory concerned, and the Company's Head Office in Amsterdam, during the

years 1856 and 1857. They are located in the section 'Incoming Correspondence (Tweede Afdeeling)' AN, Archief NHM.

14 Fernando quotes one contemporary official as remarking that 'the agreeable nature of the Javan' meant than when their headman asked for labour, they complied either out of 'apprehension or indifference'. 'Peasants and Plantation Economy', p. 10,

15 Knight, 'Peasant Labour', pp. 254–5.

16 'Residentie Banjoemas, Monographie Sf. Kaliebogor', section II, AN, Collectie Umbgrove, 10.

17 Calculations based on statistics in 'Kultuurverslag Pekalongan 1857', AN, Collectie De Vriese, 59; 'Statistiek Pekalongan 1862–1867', Exh. 20.10.1869/4 AN, Archief Kolonien 2264; 'Verslag der Statistiek Opname van Java over het Tweede Halfjaar 1869', enclosure in Governeur-General to Ministerie van Kolonien, 26.5.1870 no. 643/8, Exh. 13.7.1870/2054, AN., Archief Kolonien, 2338.

18 Robert Van Niel, R., 'The Effect of Export Cultivations in Nineteenth Century Java', *Modern Asian Studies* 15. 1 (1981), pp. 44–5 (emphasis added).

19 E.g. C. A. Bayly, 'Creating a Colonial Peasantry: India and Java *c*.1820s-1880', in M. Hasan *et al.*, *Comparative History of Indonesia*, Vol. 2 (Leiden: Brill, 1987), pp. 93–106, *Indian Society and the Making of the British Empire* (Cambridge: Cambridge University Press, 1988), pp. 136–50; Frederick Cooper, 'Peasants, Capitalists and Historians: A Review Article', *Journal of Southern African Studies* 7. 2 (1980), pp. 284–314; Jack Lewis, 'The Rise and Fall of the South African Peasantry: A Critique and Reassessment', *Journal of Southern African Studies*, 11. 1 (1984), pp. 1–24..

20 Elson aptly quotes the Resident of Kediri in 1833 on the need to settle itinerant elements in the working population: 'we can only expect useful work from them once they are settled and cultivating'. *Village Java*, p. 296.

8 Forced labourers and their resistance in Java under Japanese military rule, 1942–45

Shigeru Sato

The Japanese Army invaded Java on 1 March 1942 and occupied it until Japan's surrender in August 1945. Just before the invasion, Java had close to 50 million inhabitants and was widely considered overpopulated, with much of its population unemployed or underemployed. During the three and a half years of occupation, the Japanese launched a campaign of 'total mobilization' and drafted the local people as labourers, known as *romusha* in Japanese.[1] The scale of mobilization was massive and the work conditions were pernicious but the draftees never raised rebellions. Instead, they resorted to measures such as desertion and dereliction. This chapter analyses the reasons for the lack of open rebellions and the prevalence of passive resistance.

One obvious reason for the dearth of open rebellions would have been the power structure in which the overwhelming might of the Japanese military and the legendary docility of the Javanese peasantry constituted the two poles. This power structure alone, however, does not seem to provide a sufficient framework within which to understand the draftees' behaviour. There is little information on how this system of violence was applied to the *romusha* in Java. There are many testimonies that Japanese military men maltreated Javanese *romusha* sent outside Java. Within Java, too, there is solid evidence of Japanese brutality against looters, suspected anti-Japanese elements, and 'comfort women' among others. There is, however, no strong evidence to suggest that physical violence against the *romusha* within Java was widespread. Lack of evidence is not, of course, evidence of the lack of such violence, but there are reasons to surmise that crude violence was perhaps not necessarily ubiquitous. Within Java most of the drafted labourers were employed in civilian projects and were supervised by Japanese unarmed civilians. One Japanese overseer supervised about 1,000 labourers, which was at least ten times more workers per overseer than was normal in European enterprises in prewar Indonesia. Japanese supervisors during the occupation were much less visible to Javanese labourers than were European supervisors in the Dutch era.

The Indonesian Communist leader, Tan Malaka, assumed an alias during the occupation and looked after the *romusha* at a coalmine in West Java. In his autobiography written soon after the Japanese surrender, he warned his readers against confusing Japanese imperialism with Japanese individuals. He said that he was committed to oppose Japanese imperialism but most of the Japanese project supervisors were, although generally patriotic, nothing but ordinary company executives with technical and commercial expertise. He then described in some detail his Japanese boss who was, according to Tan Malaka, touchingly humane and did all he could to protect the well-being of the *romusha* at the cost of his own comfort.[2]

As several reports indicate that Japanese overseers in Japanese enterprises that operated in prewar Indonesia brutalized Indonesian labourers,[3] it is unlikely that Japanese overseers in Java during the occupation generally behaved as gentlemanly as Tan Malaka observed. Nevertheless lack of solid evidence prevents us from attributing labourers' sufferings to raw violence alone.

The image of docile Javanese peasants, which came to be well established during the colonial era, too, lacks strong supporting evidence. Peasant rebellions were not infrequent during the Dutch era. During the Japanese occupation also, Javanese peasants did rebel. Those rebellions were, however, not staged by draftees and were not directly related to labour mobilization. From the Dutch era there are series of reports on labourers' assaults on their overseers who maltreated them, mainly on plantations and mining sites outside of Java. Japanese civilian overseers during the occupation would have been no less vulnerable. If drafted labourers had assaulted them, the police or the military would have immediately taken retributive actions and records would have been kept, but there is no such record. As the power structure does not serve as the sole analytical framework, this chapter examines it in conjunction with the social and economic structures within which Javanese labourers had to work.

Labour and economy before the occupation

Understanding the drafted labourers' behaviour will require an analysis of their mode of existence before the war, and the way the wartime labour mobilization affected it. One characteristic of prewar Javanese society was that a substantial proportion of its population consisted of wage labourers with insufficient employment opportunities. This was partly a legacy of the world depression from 1929, which hit Java's export industries. According to the 1930 census, plantations in Java employed 8,898 European (mostly Dutch) and 966,804 Asian full-time workers.[4] The number of seasonal workers recruited from the surrounding villages was a few times larger. Together with the workers' families, several million people were dependent on the plantation sector to varying degrees. Within five years, the exportation of plantation products dropped to about one-fifth of pre-depression levels.

There are ongoing debates as to how severe the impact of the depression on Java's peasantry was, but it is certain that many employees in the export industries lost their jobs. Many small farmers lost their land and became landless.[5] Increase in landlessness meant that more people came to rely on wage labour for survival, but employment opportunities became scarcer. After 1935 the export industries showed signs of recovery, but the outbreak of the war in Europe in September 1939 dealt a new blow.

As the war spread in Europe, export industries in The Netherlands Indies again lost much of their European market. Even when markets were open, transportation became less efficient and more costly. Some cargo ships were commandeered for military purposes, the route via the Suez Canal became too perilous, and the route via the Cape of Hope cost more time and money. Moreover, increased sea perils caused marine insurance premiums to shoot up. The overall volume of exported agricultural produce thus dropped by more than 25 per cent in 1940.[6]

The impact of the European war on Javanese society was uneven. Of the export crops, sugar, coffee and tobacco were mostly located in the eastern half of the island and were heavily dependent on the European market, whereas the tea, rubber and cinchona plantations were found primarily in the western half and were less dependent on Europe. When war broke out, tea, rubber and cinchona were able to find alternative markets. Rubber in particular experienced an unprecedented boom due to increased demand from the United States. Sugar, coffee and tobacco, however, failed to find markets. The sugar plantations alone employed 55 per cent of the full-time plantation workers in 1930. Consequently, unemployment and destitution became markedly more serious in the eastern half, which roughly corresponded to the area that had supplied many wage labourers to the export industries.[7]

The changes in the international arena prompted changes in domestic economic policies that affected day-to-day lives of Java's peasants. When war became imminent in Europe, the Dutch colonial authorities started economic preparations, one aspect of which was a control of food distribution. During the heyday of the colonial era when the export industries rapidly grew, The Netherlands Indies began importing much rice from the river delta regions of mainland Southeast Asia. During the early 1930s, the price of all export crops including rice dropped, and importation of cheap rice from mainland Southeast Asia started harming Indonesian rice farmers. As a protective measure, the Dutch authorities restricted the importation of rice, and designated Java as the main supplier of rice to deficit areas within the Indies. Java's rice growers were thus protected but at the cost of the domestic consumers, particularly wage labourers whose wages dropped and whose job opportunities dwindled but who still had to pay an artificially high price for rice.[8]

Within Java, the Dutch instituted stronger measures to control rice distribution and obliged rice mills to sell all processed rice to the government. This control measure, however, resulted in economic compartmentalization along the lines of administrative boundaries, and hampered the natural flow of rice from the surplus to the deficit areas. This problem became more pronounced during the Japanese occupation.[9]

Curiously enough, most historical studies of Indonesian economy in the so-called 'late colonial era' end in 1939, treating the final few years as if they had not really existed. Contemporary sources however inform us that the health conditions of the people deteriorated markedly after 1939. Cases of disease associated with malnourishment, such as hunger oedema, increased. Rising death rates surpassed declining birth rates in certain regencies. Some people who lost their livelihood in the countryside migrated to the cities where, failing to find other ways of earning a living, many resorted to begging and prostitution. This led to further social disruption and increased rates of venereal disease. A resultant moral collapse also worried Indonesian intellectuals.[10]

Javanese society was already suffering when the Japanese invasion landed another heavy blow. The most serious effect of the occupation was the nearly complete halt of the normal international and inter-island trading, in favour of a much-reduced exchange of commodities controlled by the occupation forces. This was a crushing blow to the plantations, which had to lay off most of their employees. Some workers were retained for maintenance jobs but their wages dropped. All this meant that, at the beginning of the occupation, Java had large cohorts of wage labourers who desperately needed job opportunities.

Economic change and labour mobilization during the occupation

Creating jobs for the unemployed was one of the earliest tasks for the Japanese occupation authorities. In August 1942, Jakarta authorities appointed Japanese administrative staff to the 17 residencies and two principalities in Java. Some of these administrators started relief works in their jurisdictions. Until late 1943 the largest work project was the rehabilitation of Java's infrastructure that the retreating Dutch had destroyed in scorched-earth tactics.[11] Many railway and road bridges, harbour facilities and factories had to be restored. At this stage, the Japanese treated labour mobilization and wages as classified information, so there are few records. They apparently recruited labour through Indonesian local government officials on an ad hoc basis. Judging from the wage regulations announced later, the wages they paid were probably comparable with the standard wages immediately before the Japanese invasion, which were very low.

Politically, many Indonesians rejoiced to see the Japanese invading forces drive out Indonesia's former colonial masters. Economically, too, the rehabilitation would have been a welcome move. The scale of labour mobilization for this project was, however, much smaller than the amount of unemployment that the war and occupation created. The Indonesian intellectuals who acted as the advisers to the occupation government kept arguing until late 1943 that unemployment was the most serious social and economic problem and required urgent attention of the occupation authorities.[12]

From the outset of their war effort, the Japanese advocated the necessity of 'total mobilization' of manpower for what they conceived as a 'total war'. In the first half of occupation, their advocacy was little more than a mere slogan. In the second half, they implemented it almost to the letter, which created 'shortages' of labour throughout the 'overpopulated' island of Java. Tokyo authorities in the middle of 1943 initiated this change because a series of major defeats in the Pacific battlefront compelled them to alter Japan's military and economic strategies.

The war theatre had been overstretched. Japan's military leaders therefore drew a line well behind the existing battlefront that they called 'the absolute national defence line'. Japan's war effort along this line required labour mobilization, which became an onerous burden on the communities in the vicinity. Java, being away from the battlefront, experienced no battles during much of the occupation and, although it supplied labour to the front, this comprised a small fraction of the total workforce drafted in Java. Within Java as well, the share of labour mobilized for military projects, including production of strategically important items, was small in comparison with that drafted for economic projects.

In the economic field, the major policy change was a shift from the construction of a 'Greater East Asia Co-Prosperity Sphere' to the formation of many smaller autarkic units within the occupied area. Tokyo authorities never produced detailed economic plans for their much-vaunted 'Co-Prosperity Sphere', a vague concept in which the aim was to build an industrial core in the north, comprising Japan, Manchukuo and northern China, and to secure the 'Southern Regions' as suppliers of raw materials and as markets for the industrial goods. They therefore did not envisage industrialization in occupied Southeast Asia. Their scheme was, however, soon shattered by the Allied counter-offensives, which effectively cut the transportation lines between the south and north. There followed another scheme which included 'industrialization' in each of the smaller occupied units, such as Java. The purpose of industrialization was not so much to boost Japan's war potential or enrich the occupied area than to enable each area to survive in isolation.[13] It was this makeshift economic measure for survival that demanded the massive manpower mobilization in Java.

Quick establishment of economic self-sufficiency in Java required urgent production of import substitutes and complex economic restructuring. However, the 'Co-Prosperity Sphere' was economically unviable from the outset as it lacked certain resources. For instance, in order to produce basic commodities like clothes, cotton had to be imported from India or the US and wool from Australia.[14] Japan also had insufficient purchasing power to afford to procure the abundant tropical products. Military reverses, when they arrived, made these problems more acute.

Despite the euphemism of 'Co-Prosperity', it was obvious that the military occupation would result in serious economic disruptions in the occupied territory. Japanese authorities initially planned to keep Indonesia as a permanent part of the Japanese Empire. As the economic conditions deteriorated, however, the Japanese grudgingly came to deem it necessary to make some political concessions, particularly in the form of a promise of national independence in the future. While granting piecemeal political concessions, the authorities also made economic reform plans and assigned projects to Japanese companies. Although these companies dispatched their staff to the occupied territories, the authorities in Jakarta set production quotas for all projects in Java. The company staff then calculated the labour requirement for each assigned project and submitted a request for labour to Jakarta. Jakarta coordinated demand and supply and issued labour mobilization quotas to the villages via the administrative network, which was expanded to accommodate a 'labour section' at all levels.[15]

The projects were numerous and the production quotas were high – reflecting the enormity of the economic problems that the war had created. Even though 'total mobilization' was implemented, the authorities were rarely able to supply the requested amounts of labour for the new projects. The project coordinators had to fulfil the production quotas by the set dates with insufficient labour, equipment or expertise. The Japanese were constantly reminded that the survival of the whole (Japanese) nation was at stake. They therefore drove the workers extremely hard, often round the clock, adopting a two-shift or three-shift system. They placed the utmost priority on output, often neglecting contingent matters such as provision of food, clothing, accommodation and medical care to the labourers.[16]

In prewar Indonesia harsh work conditions had been observed when demands of labour increased rapidly and preparation of housing, medical care and other supporting facilities lagged behind.[17] The war and occupation created a similar situation but on a larger scale and more rapidly. To justify the harsh work conditions, the Japanese propaganda machine broadcast to the local population the idea that their historic mission to liberate Asians from Western oppression could not be achieved without sacrifice, and that the Japanese were taking the initiative by willingly sacrificing their own lives for the cause.

Open rebellions and passive resistance

Work conditions plummeted but the draftees never rebelled. To understand the absence of open rebellions by draftees, it will be useful to examine the rebellions that did take place. The second half of the occupation witnessed three uprisings large enough to alarm the Japanese.

The first broke out on 25 February 1944 in Singaparna Village in West Java, led by a local Muslim teacher, Kiai Zainal Mustofa. After the outbreak of the European war, Mustofa was imprisoned twice by the Dutch for leading anti-Dutch campaigns. Seeing that the Japanese too were oppressive and exploitative, he instigated his followers to an armed uprising against the new foreign invaders. Before the uprising was launched, however, the Japanese military received intelligence and sent four military policemen to the mosque during the prayer gathering on Friday 24 February 1944. A brawl ensued in which three Japanese were killed and one escaped. The following day, the Japanese sent in the army, killed 86 people and arrested between 700 and 800. They sentenced to death 23 arrestees including Mustofa, imprisoned 79 and released the rest.[18]

The second uprising took place in April 1944 in the regency of Indramayu, a major rice-growing region in West Java. It was apparently a spontaneous riot by rice-growing farmers against the compulsory delivery of rice to the government. The riot broke out in a village when the authorities tried to prevent a large landholder from selling his crop on the black market. Although the riot in that village was swiftly quelled, it spread to other parts of the regency and continued for about four months until the end of the harvesting season. The ending was particularly bloody with the army shooting to death hundreds of rioters.[19]

The third uprising was launched on 14 February 1945 in Blitar regency in East Java by one of the battalions of the indigenous defence forces that the Japanese created throughout Java. The rebels, who were professionally trained, organized and equipped, launched surprise attacks in which they managed to kill a few Japanese, but Japanese forces swiftly overpowered them. The battalion's commander, Supriyadi, was probably captured and executed. The Indonesian nationalists, however, came to regard him as an embodiment of the spirit of their struggle, refused to accept his death, and on 5 October 1945, appointed him in absentia Defence Minister of the newly born Republic of Indonesia.[20]

Apparently none of the leaders of the above rebellions publicly announced the causes of their actions. Since all the three uprisings broke out in the second half of the occupation when the people's living standard markedly deteriorated, we might surmise that the economic deterioration constituted the common background. The economic plight of the people was, however, not a sufficient condition for rebellions. The drafted labourers experienced much worse conditions but they never rebelled. In addition to worsened living conditions, the rebels were motivated by other forces, such as religious or political ideology and the prospect of winning economic gains.

The peasant riot in Indramayu involved the largest number of casualties, and may look on the surface to have been a futile and costly attempt. The peasantry in Indramayu, however, did win substantial economic gains after making so many sacrifices. Indramayu was a major rice surplus area. The economic compartmentalization along the administrative boundaries resulted in a fall in the price of rice.[21] The government gradually raised the official purchasing price of harvested rice, but due to the wartime inflation, the official price soon became less attractive. For the rice growers in Indramayu to gain decent profits, they had to violate the government regulations and shift their produce to deficit regencies where rice fetched higher prices on the black market. A conflict of interests emerged between the farmers and the local government officials. Although the occupation authorities quelled the riots in a brutal manner, they subsequently lowered the delivery quota for Indramayu by about 45 per cent, which meant that the farmers in Indramayu became able to sell most of their produce on the black market.[22] This was a major victory for the local farmers as well as for the landless peasants who were dependent on the landed farmers.

In comparison with those who rebelled, the drafted labourers lacked a guiding ideology, training for fighting, or the prospect to obtain any real gain through rebellions. Instead of rebelling, they resorted to passive resistance, of which desertion was the most prevalent form. It was particularly frequent when labourers received advance payment of their wages.[23] Advance payment obviously gave the workers a temptation to abscond before working, but the Japanese (like Europeans before the war) adopted it because it had been a widely used, proven method for quick and large-scale labour recruitment, and an excuse for recapturing deserters.

The Japanese transported many labourers by rail from the impoverished East and Central Java to West Java where they conducted a number of large construction projects. This method of transportation facilitated desertion. Taking a train was a new experience for most draftees. When the train started moving towards an unknown destination, some were so scared that they jumped off the moving train and injured or killed themselves. Java's railways were mostly single-track, and trains had to stop frequently to wait for the trains running in the opposite direction. Most trains operated only in daytime. A train trip from the eastern end to the western end of Java thus took a few days. Every time a train stopped, some draftees escaped, and by the time it reached the destination, often a third or more had already left.[24]

At large construction sites, the Japanese conducted medical check-ups of the draftees before and after the consigned period of work, in an attempt to keep the labour's 'attrition rate' low, and to prevent infectious diseases from spreading. In the initial check-ups, many draftees were found to have infectious diseases or be otherwise unfit for work, and were sent back to their original villages. In some cases the Japanese conducted pre-work immunization of the draftees. Modern medical treatment, such as injection, was alien to most of Java's rural population. They were so frightened of injections that the authorities had to discontinue immunization in some cases.[25] They also set up clinics at large work sites. The draftees were scared of the clinics, and often preferred to abscond to being admitted to a dreaded clinic, popularly known as death houses.[26]

Fear of ghosts and other supernatural beings also contributed to the frequency of flight. When someone died in a workers' barrack, others in the same barrack often disappeared at night en masse, apparently frightened of the presence of the ghost of the dead.[27] The Javanese also believed that ghosts or some other scary supernatural creatures inhabited certain areas. When projects were conducted in such areas, desertion rates became high. Those places often coincided with malarial areas. Undernourishment lowered the workers' stamina and immunity, and made them vulnerable to a range of diseases such as malaria, dysentery, yaws, tropical ulcer and gangrene.

The Allied Forces, who observed Japanese activities in Java via aerial photographs and other means, tried to destroy some Japanese construction projects by bombing. They knew, however, that a more effective way to frustrate the Japanese projects was to make the workers desert the work sites. They therefore dropped leaflets urging Indonesian workers to run away as bombing was imminent. Such leaflets were more effective weapons than the bombs, reported an Allied intelligence officer.[28]

The Japanese in Java had few effective means to reduce desertion rates. A physical escape, however, did not mean an escape from suffering. It often was the beginning of further suffering. Many workers escaped after sustaining injuries or contracting diseases. After escaping, their illnesses aggravated, and many died during the flight. If escapees were to walk from West Java to their home in Central or East Java, it would take them many days or weeks. Those draftees spoke Javanese and did not understand Sundanese spoken in West Java; even asking directions was difficult for them. Many became lost in the midst of their own homeland, soon exhausted what money they had, and died from hunger and illness.[29]

Escape from misery but where to?

In the Dutch era also, labourers' desertion from export enterprises was a common phenomenon. When work conditions were poor, ten per cent or more workers deserted even when work sites were in remote areas and the chance of survival outside the premises was practically nil.[30] The methods of labour recruitment also contributed to high desertion rate. Until the depression in the 1930s most labourers worked on a contract, and desertion was punishable. Contract labourers were, however, often not properly informed of the work conditions or even the destinations. Most villagers in Java were generally reluctant to commit themselves to work outside of Java or their villages. In order to recruit large numbers of labourers swiftly in this situation, deception and compulsion were commonly used. During the depression the system of 'contract labour' was replaced by 'free labour', but deception and compulsion persisted.[31]

The Japanese replaced the 'free' recruitment with a quota system using the bureaucratic network. People's reluctance to be sent away persisted. So did the deception and compulsion in recruiting, albeit by different agents. Disobeying the traditional authorities was difficult for the village poor, particularly during the occupation since prices of food rose while employment opportunities within the villages diminished. Moreover, most of the Japanese projects were designed to mitigate the economic difficulties of wartime. Economic conditions, nevertheless, continued to deteriorate as did work conditions. The *romusha* generally had a starvation diet because the Japanese rice policy, based on 'production increase' and forced delivery to the government, created chaos and the occupation authorities failed to secure enough food for the labourers they drafted.

In the course of 1944, it became painfully obvious even to Japanese eyes that the 'total mobilization' of labour was excessive, having a gravely negative impact on Javanese society. At the end of 1944 the occupation authorities therefore suspended most of their military projects and concentrated on the campaign of 'production increase', particularly of food and clothing for the local population.

The campaign proved counterproductive. As the campaign intensified, production of food crops dropped sharply. Many farmers abandoned farming because the labour mobilization depleted labour from the farming sector. Irrigation networks suffered from disrepair. The incentives to farm diminished because of runaway currency inflation which devalued the official purchase price of farm produce. Moreover, forcible cultivation of non-edible crops such as cotton, required to produce clothes, took up much of the farmland. By early 1945, the lowering of physical stamina amongst the rural population had become unmistakably visible. Many *romusha* became too ill to work, and attendance on work sites dropped to as low as 40 per cent in some cases.[32]

The desertion rate rose. Work sites in Java were usually in the proximity of local communities, which also facilitated desertion. Surviving after desertion was however by no means easy. Even if deserters managed to reach their home villages, there was no guarantee that their plight would subside. Much of the labour was drafted from low strata of rural communities. As employment opportunities in the villages dwindled, landless peasants had to seek livelihood elsewhere, which usually meant to be recruited as *romusha*, or alternatively, migrate to the cities hoping to find some means of survival.

The cities swelled with migrants from the countryside. The population of Jakarta rose by over 40 per cent during the occupation, from 594,000 to 844,000.[33] The Japanese decided to mobilize the urban homeless too as *romusha*. According to newspaper reports, on the morning of 5 February 1945 the police in Jakarta City began hunting for the homeless in the dark and by dawn rounded up 931 people of working ages, consisting of 792 men and 139 women. Physical check-ups revealed that 387 men (49%) and 90 women (65%) were unfit for work due to malnourishment and illnesses. The Japanese provided them with some food and medicines, and put them to work as soon as they appeared to be physically able.[34]

A novel written soon after the Japanese surrender by the renowned author, Pramoedya Ananta Toer, describes the final stage of occupation as follows, from the point of view of a village chief:

When you go to the city you see children sprawled lifeless at the side of the road. In front of the market and the stores, down beneath the bridge, on top of garbage heaps and in the gutters there are corpses. Nothing but corpses. The place is filled with the dead – children and the old people. And you know what they do? If they are going to die, before they take their final breath, they first gather a pile of teakwood or banana leaves that have been used to wrap food in. And they cover their bodies with those leaves and they die. It's like they know that in two hours they're going to die and that after they are dead no one is going to prepare them for burial. These are crazy times we're going through. And I don't know why it is. In all my life this is the first time I've seen anything like it. Corpses. Wherever you go, unattended corpses.[35]

In Pramoedya's novel the countryside was also filled with the destitute. The village chief made a fortune by smuggling teak, which the Japanese needed in large quantities as construction timber and fuel for locomotives. When the chief held a circumcision rite for his son, beggars swarmed to it. The son said to his mother: 'Why don't you give them something, Mother?' The mother replied: 'These days, there are thousands of them around. They are like ants. And if you pay any attention at all . . . '.[36]

After the surrender, the occupation authorities submitted to the Allied forces a summary report on the social and economic conditions in Java, stating that the people were generally malnourished, their physical power and will-power were low, their labour capacity inferior, and in certain regions chronic malaria, venereal disease, skin disease and hunger oedema were spreading at an extraordinary rate among the village poor.[37]

From 23 January to 3 February 1946, the Dutch military intelligence corps that accompanied the British forces conducted an inspection into the general situation of the health and food supply of people in the Sukabumi regency. According to their report, starvation and disease were rife in the rural districts, and the hospitals were under-staffed and badly stocked. The British began providing the destitute with some medical aid and food, one mess tin full of rice per person per day. The number of people who appeared for the rice grew from 60–100 to 700–800 daily, some coming from 20 to 30 miles away. Cases occurred of people dying whilst waiting for assistance near the camp. This aid, however, had to cease as the British moved to another city.[38]

The peasantry of Java desperately needed help but there was no assistance to be had during the war. The Japanese kept pushing for 'total mobilization', although they knew that their efforts were counterproductive. Indonesian nationalist leaders, although they continually expressed concerns about the welfare of the people, were powerless to improve the economic situation. More concerned with preparing their nation for the political independence that Japan had promised to grant, they generally cooperated with the Japanese, as did other indigenous leaders. Daily essentials became steadily less available and prices rose beyond the reach of the poor. Those who did earn money found it continuously undermined by currency inflation. Under such circumstances, the only mode of resistance open to drafted workers was to walk away, even though it often meant for them to walk into further suffering, and death.

Forced labourers might not have had a systematic and comprehensive understanding of the situation in which they found themselves during the occupation, but they no doubt knew that open rebellion or revolt would not influence the overall situation in any substantial way because the Japanese military possessed superior power. However, when Japan surrendered and the forced labour recruitment ended, people in Java's countryside started launching assaults on the local government officials and wealthy ethnic Chinese who had acted as agents of the Japanese. During the occupation, local officials had ordered the villagers to surrender their labour and rice to the Japanese while Chinese rice dealers, through black-marketeering often practised with the collusion of government officials, had accumulated wealth while villagers starved. Although former *romusha* as such did not act collectively, most non-elite villagers had been forced to work for the Japanese at various stages and felt great resentment about how they had been treated during the war. It was only after the power structure altered and the agents of the power holders were no longer protected that the villagers' anger came out into the open and was directed to these agents, seeking 'justice' (*kedaulatan*).[39]

Notes

1 For a general treatment of this topic see Shigeru Sato, 'Forced Labour Mobilization in Java during the Second World War', *Slavery & Aboliton*, 24. 2 (2003), pp. 97–110.

2 Tan Malaka, *Dari Pendjara ke Pendjar* [From Prison to Prison] (Jakarta: Widaya, 1947–48), vol. 2, pp. 158–9.

3 Vincent J. H. Houben, J. Thomas Lindblad *et al.*, *Coolie Labour in Colonial Indonesia: A Study of Labour Relations in the Outer Islands, c.1900–1940* (Wiesbaden: Harrassowitz Verlag, 1999), pp. 119, 168–70.

4 *Indisch Verslag 1941: Statistisch Jaaroverzicht van Nederlandisch-Indië over het Jaar 1940, Netherlands Indian Report 1941, Statistical Report for the Year 1940* (Batavia: Centraal Kantoor voor de Statistiek van het Department van Economische Zaken, 1941), pp. 177–80.

5 For recent surveys see Peter Boomgaard and Ian Brown (eds), *Weathering the Storm: The Economies of Southeast Asia during the 1930s Depression* (Leiden: KITLV Press; Singapore: Institute of Southeast Asian Studies, 2000), particularly chapter 2, pp. 23–52, and Peter Boomgaard, 'Labour in Java in the 1930s', CLARA Working Papers on Asian Labour, no. 7, Amsterdam: International Institute of Social History, 1999.

6 *Indisch Verslag 1941*, pp. 355, 360.

7 *Voedselproblemen en Overheidspolitiek op Java en Madoera* [Food Problems and the Government Policies in Java and Madura] *Koloniaal Tijdschrift* [Colonial Review], 29e jaargang (December 1940), pp. 643–55.

8 Ibid., pp. 673–89.

9 Ibid., pp. 677–84; and 'Rijstpellerijen in Midden-Java gedurende Japansche Bezetting' [Rice Mills in Central Java during the Japanese Occupation], *Economisch Weekblad voor Nederlandsch-Indië* [Economic Weekly for The Netherlands Indies], 21 (3 August 1946), pp. 161–3.

10 For the medical aspects, see Dr Boentaran Martoatmodjo's article in *Berita Ketabitan: Madjallah dari Djawa Izi Hookoo Kai* [Medial Report: Journal of the Java Medical Service Association], 4–6 (1944) – in BUZA (The Dutch Ministry of Foreign Affairs), NEFIS/CMI bijlage 3, 2475. For Indonesian intellectuals' observations and views, see the series of discussion in 'Panitia Adat dan Tatanegara Dahoeloe: Bahagian Kesedjahatraan dan Kemakmoeran' [The Committee to Investigate Old Customs and Institutions: Division of Welfare and Prosperity], BUZA NEFIS/CMI, bijlage 3, 2241.

11 'Kokyo Shisetsu no Gaikyo' [Outline of the Public Works], BUZA NEFIS/CMI, bijlage 3, 1776 and 2048.

12 'Panitia Adat dan Tatanegara Dahoeloe', BUZA NEFIS/CMI, bijlage 3, 2241.

13 The key documents are: 'Nanpo Keizai Taisaku Yoko' [The Economic Policies in the Southern Regions], adopted on 12 December 1941; and 'Nanpo Keizai Rikugun Shori Yoryo' [Guidelines for the Army's Economic Administration in the Southern Regions], adopted on 5 June 1943, in *Shiryo Shu Nanpo no Gunsei* [Collected Documents on the Military Administration in the Southern Regions] (Tokyo: Asagumo Shinbunsha, 1985), pp. 129–36, 159–67.

14 For more detail see Shigeru Sato, 'Japanisation in Indonesia Re-Examined: the Problem of Self-Sufficiency in Clothing', in Li Narangoa and Robert Cribb (eds), *Imperial Japan and National Identities in Asia, 1895–1945* (Richmond: Curzon Press, 2003), pp. 350–76.

15 'List of the Companies That Have Been Operating in Java During The War, By Order of The Japanese Military Administration HQ', BUZA NEFIS/CMI, bijlage 3, 2398; *Garis-Garis Besar Pengerahan Romusha* [Guidelines for *Romusha* Mobilization], (Jakarta, n.d.).

16 *Jawa Rikuyu Sokyoku Shi* [History of the General Land Transportation Bureau in Java] (Tokyo: Jawa Rikuyu Sokyoku Shi Kankokai, 1976), pp. 250–1.

17 Houben *et al.*, *Coolie Labour in Colonial Indonesia*, pp. 165–6.

18 Goto, Ken'ichi, *Nippon Senryoki Indoneshia Kenkyu* [Studies of Indonesia during the Japanese Occupation] (Tokyo: Ryukei Shosha, 1989), pp. 109–48; Kurasawa, Aiko, *Nippon Senryo ka Jawa Noson no Henyo* [Transformation of Village Java under the Japanese Occupation] (Tokyo: Soshi Sha, 1992), pp. 471–86.

19 Aiko Kurasawa, 'Forced Delivery of Paddy and Peasant Uprising in Indramayu: Japanese Occupation and Social Change', *Developing Economies*, 21. 1 (March 1983), pp. 52–72; Shigeru Sato, 'The Pangreh Praja in Java under Japanese Military Rule', *Bijdragen tot de Taal-, Land- en Volkenkunde*, 152. 4 (1996), pp. 586–608.

20 Nugroho Notosusanto, *The Peta Army during the Japanese Occupation of Indonesia* (Tokyo: Waseda University Press, 1979).

21 *Asia Raya* [Greater Asia – an Indonesian daily published in Java], 19 May and 3 June 1942.

22 The delivery quota for the Residency of Cirebon (in which Indramayu regency was the main rice-producing area) was lowered from 168,000 tonnes to 92,000 tonnes.

23 *Jawa Rikuyu Sokyoku Shi*, p. 256.

24 Tan Malaka, *Dari Pendjara ke Pendjara*, vol. 2, pp. 154–6.

25 'Rapport Inzake Werving en Transport van Romusha's in de Residentie Semarang' [Report on Recruitment and Transport of *Romusha* in the Residency of Semarang], BUZA NEFIS/CMI, bijlage 3, 3535.

26 Aiko Kurasawa, 'Mobilization and Control: A Study of Social Change in Rural Java, 1942–1945', PhD thesis, Cornell University, 1989, pp. 194, 225.
27 *Jawa Rikuyu Sokyoku Shi*, pp. 255–6.
28 'Economic (Mining) Targets in the N.E.I.', 30 December 1944, BUZA NEFIS/CMI, deel 1, 1784, p. 24.
29 Tan Malaka, *Dari Pendjara ke Pendjara*, vol. 2, p. 166.
30 Houben *et al.*, *Coolie Labour in Colonial Indonesia*, p.166
31 Ibid., particularly ch. 2.
32 *Jawashinbun* ['*Java Daily*'], 7 June 1945.
33 NIOD IC (The Netherlands Institute for War Documentation, Indonesian Collection) 005309.
34 *Jawashiunbun*, 6 February 1945.
35 Pramoedya Ananta Toer, *The Fugitive*, translated by Willem Samuel (New York: Penguin Books, 1990), p. 33.
36 Ibid. p. 13.
37 'Personnel', NIOD IC, 012221.
38 'Report on the General Situation Regarding the Health of the Inhabitants of Soekaboemi Area', 19 February 1946, p. 3 – NA (The Dutch National Archive), ASB 3371.
39 See for a detailed case study Anton Lucas, *One Soul One Struggle: Region and Revolution in Indonesia* (Sydney: Allen & Unwin, 1991).

9 'Unfree' labour on the cattle stations of Northern Australia, the tea gardens of Assam and the rubber plantations of Indo-China, 1920–50

Robert Castle, James Hagan and Andrew Wells*

This chapter examines unfree labour in three industries in the nineteenth and early twentieth century. It focuses on the forms and consequences of protest which arose amongst workers in these industries in response to the conditions under which they were employed. The Assamese tea industry, Vietnamese rubber plantations and Northern Australian cattle ranching used differing means of production, technology and investment but all relied on colonial governments to enable them to recruit and retain a 'contracted' labour force. The forms of the labour relationship varied but led to protests which often took on a wider meaning in struggles for liberation.

Assam

British investment in Assam produced the 'tea mania' of the 1860s, and it continued to grow almost without interruption until the 1940s. The tea firms had their headquarters in London, and they enjoyed the support of governments whose imperial policies included the domination of the world tea market.[1] The tea gardens were very profitable. In 1939, when the average yield on British Bonds was about 4 per cent, tea firms operating in Assam paid an average of 15 per cent. In 1942, 197 of the 255 tea companies in Assam paid 28 per cent or better.[2]

Tea growing technology did not change between 1860 and 1940. The industry remained labour-intensive, and the tea companies were able to amass their profits by keeping labour costs down. Wages in the tea gardens remained well below those paid to labourers working outside them.[3] The planters' method was to recruit labourers in some distant province and bring them to Assam under indentures. The indentures they signed, or put thumbprint to, provided for wages and conditions for a set period (usually three, sometimes five years) and allowed for no variation in the cost of living. If labourers left their employer during that period, then they were subject to penalties, which included jailing with hard labour.

In 1906, a committee of inquiry concluded that the current system of recruitment under indenture would not be able to supply all the labour that tea plantations required for their continued expansion. Following its recommendations, a Labour Board composed mainly of tea planters managed the supply of labour to the tea gardens. Planters lost their right to the private arrest of absconding coolies, and the laws which punished breach of indenture as a criminal offence were gradually repealed, the last of them in 1925. At that time, there were still over 120,000 coolies working in the gardens who had been brought to Assam under indenture.[4]

The decision to repeal the last laws treating a breach of indenture as a criminal offence was a result of the recommendation of a committee inquiring into the strike of over 200,000 coolies in the Chargola and Surma Valleys in 1918. Until then, conditions in the tea gardens had not provoked collective protest. Wages were chronically low, food often poor, housing inadequate and discipline brutal, but protest had been personal or confined to a small group on one garden. The most common form of protest was to abscond, but self-mutilation was well known, and attacks on overseers and managers occurred frequently. There was a kind of collective response in that the coolies failed to reproduce themselves, but this was hardly designed to achieve an industrial purpose.[5]

In 1918, famine increased the supply of labourers available to the Labour Board, and dramatically increased the number transported to Assam. Famine also increased the price of food, but wages remained the same, or went down.[6] Nationalist Congress agitators urged the coolies to demand higher wages, and if they did not get them, to return to the simple life their villages had provided. A few days later, the coolies left the gardens, many of them shouting 'Gandhi Mahary Sri Tai' ('Hail Gandhi').[7] At the railway stations, officials acting under government orders refused to sell the coolies tickets, even though public subscriptions had provided them with money for their fares. On the night of 20 May, the 3,000 coolies stranded at Chadpur were suddenly baton-charged and flogged. The next day, Gurkhas with fixed bayonets attacked the coolies while they were sleeping. An official estimate was that '300 people died owing, perhaps, to police action and cholera'.[8]

In November 1921, the Government of Assam established a committee to inquire into the conditions of coolie labour in the tea gardens. It found that the strikes had been the work of 'non-co-operation and other agitators'. It did not recommend an increase in wages, but it did recommend the repeal of the Workmans' Breach of Contract Act.[9] After the Government of India repealed this Act in 1925, all tea garden coolies could legally withdraw their labour. Seven years later, the Tea Districts Emigrant Labour Act confirmed the labourer's right of repatriation at the employer's expense.

These were important additions to the coolies' power in law to bargain freely over wages and conditions. In practice, they were heavily offset by other circumstances. The first of these was the changing nature of the supply of labour. By the 1890s, some planters were attempting to secure their labour supply by offering land to coolies who had served out their contract. The Government of Assam reinforced this policy by making land available for the same purpose. By 1926–27 this policy had succeeded to the extent that about 65 per cent of the new labourers engaged to work in the tea gardens were born in Assam. By 1930, according to one estimate, there were 600,000 ex-garden labourers settled on government land.[10]

Despite this addition of locally born labour, Assam remained a large importer of coolies, even when the acreage under tea declined during the Great Depression, and the Government of India restricted the export of tea in the post-Depression years. The Act which guaranteed the tea labourers' right of repatriation also abolished the Labour Board, allowed the deregulation of restricted recruiting areas, and established a Controller under whose supervision migration was to continue. The Act's theory was that 'the great supply [of labour would remove] the need for control and when more people offered for recruitment than could be accepted, the necessity for control should disappear entirely'.[11] By 1934, the Government recognized that 'much more labour was available than could be accepted', but in that year 48,000 coolies migrated to Assam, and an average of about 25,000 arrived each year until 1940.[12]

Oversupply severely limited the coolies' power to bargain. So did the collusive practices of the planters. Members of the Indian Tea Association were required not to offer wage rises without first consulting the Association.[13] Locally, they enforced their wage agreements through 'District' or 'Circle' Committees. If a labourer wished to move from one garden to another, he had to present a reference from his former employer; and a transfer fee applied.[14] But, as the 1946 Enquiry noted, 'In actual practice the labourer did not feel free to move'.[15] One reason for this was that the practice of taking a thumbprint for receipt of the 'bonus' at the end of the engagement gave coolies, unaware of their legal rights, the impression that they were still under contract. Another was the presence of the *chaukidar*, who acted as a watchman to see that they did not leave the plantation, or receive unauthorized visitors. Planters insisted on their rights as owners of private property to deny entry to any person who did not have their permission.[16] Attempts in the Assam Legislature to open tea gardens to public access failed.[17] Within the gardens, planters permitted meetings only for religious purposes.

Limits on free association made the organization of effective industrial action almost impossible. Besides prohibition of access there were other serious difficulties. The tea plantation coolies came from several different regions in India. They differed in religion and culture, and they lacked a common language. Overcoming these problems was beyond the resources of the infant trade union movement. Although the All-India Trade Union Congress dated from 1920, India's 343 registered unions in 1938 still only had a combined membership of 390,000.[18] A registered union did not appear in the gardens until 1939, and apparently did not last long. The

1946 Enquiry noted that there was only one 'functioning' trade union operating in the Assam gardens. Its organization was limited to a few gardens, and it had about 900 members – out of a workforce of over one million.[19]

Despite lack of trade union organization, there were still strikes, at least 115 of them in the years 1930 to 1939, involving as many as 5,900 labourers during 1934, and not less than about 2,000 in any one year. Some were 'protests against ill-treatment', others were the result of 'economic grievances, including demands for higher wages'.[20] None of them succeeded in having any significant effect on wage rates. In 1946, the daily wage rates of agricultural workers in Assam were still 'much higher than the average daily wages of labourers in tea gardens'.[21] This remained true even after due allowance had been made for subsidized food and accommodation in the gardens.[22]

In the judgement of the 1946 Enquiry, the Assam Government had not helped the coolies in their quest for higher wages. It was not interested in the merits of strikes, but only in keeping the peace, and maintaining the status quo.[23] It did not act on a recommendation from the Royal Commission of 1929–31 that it establish a statutory body to fix a minimum wage. Nor did the Government act on a series of detailed recommendations in the Commission's Report for the improvement in coolie housing on the estates. Its one response to the Commission's many suggestions for increasing the freedom of coolie workers and improving their conditions of employment was to appoint officials to inspect the gardens biennially. The 1946 Enquiry reported that

> As there is no statutory authority for these inspections, they have no binding force. It appears, however, that all these Inspecting Officers rarely talk with the labourers privately, that is without the presence of the manager or supervisor, and that they collect the necessary information from the managers themselves.[24]

It was information so gathered that allowed the Honourable Sir Frank Noyce to state in answer to a question in the Legislative Assembly that, 'There is no reason to believe that the conditions of labourers in the Assam tea estates was not satisfactory'[25]. He was aware that some of the recommendations of the Royal Commission had not been carried out, but 'Assam was not a wealthy province'.[26]

Vietnam

In 1902, Governor General Paul Doumer promulgated the first budget for the colony of Cochinchina and the Protectorates of Tonkin and Annam. The French had established their commercial and political control in Vietnam through military intervention, and then signed a series of treaties with the existing rulers. Doumer had imposed an administrative system with some provincial autonomy, but concentrated in his hands all matters relating to Indochina's relationship with Metropolitan France.[27] Indochina was to supply France with food and raw materials in an imperial regime of free trade.

French investment, channelled through imperial banks, was concentrated in mining (mainly coal), and agriculture – originally rice, and then rubber. Much of the agricultural and plantation activity was located in the more entrepreneurial frontier economy of Cochinchina (extending into Cambodia). Indochina did not develop any secondary industries that could have absorbed the surplus population of the crowded Red River delta area of Tonkin.[28] That area supplied labour for French extractive and agricultural enterprises for the land that they had expropriated and parcelled out to *colons* in 'concessions'.[29]

Full exploitation of the land required infrastructure work: drainage, dykes, canals, roads, railways, as well as military and police forces to preserve law and order. To finance these works, the French reformed the administrative system and traditional methods of gathering revenue. Amending the communal system of taxation, the French levied individuals in money. The village head organized taxes for the entire village and individuals unable to meet their personal assessment incurred debt.[30] The French also raised revenue through government monopolies on salt, opium and alcohol.[31] Taxation exacerbated class tensions in the densely populated Red River delta and helped generate a supply of labour available for mines and southern rubber and rice plantations.[32]

Rubber plantations were established in 1906 in the 'grey lands', fairly close to Saigon, employing local village labour. By 1915 Indochina produced 298 tons of rubber on 15,000 hectares of plantations.[33] After 1920, 'rubber mania' followed. Within a decade 100,000 hectares were planted, and the rubber harvest exceeded 10,000 tons.[34] The stimulus was high profits through supplying rubber for electrical insulation and vehicle tyres. Rubber prices escalated from 16 US cents per pound in 1920 to 73 cents per pound in 1925.

The new plantations were established on the 'red lands', a 50-kilometres arc stretching from the southeast to northwest of Saigon. The indigenous Trieng and Mois were deemed unsuitable by the planters for work: they would only attend work when they felt like it, and often went home to their families at night, rather than camp on site ready for an early start the next day.[35] Clearing the jungle was labour intensive. The work was heavy and dangerous and malaria alone caused thousands of deaths on the 'red land' plantations.[36] The planters' solution to the problem of labour supply was to import indentured workers from the overcrowded cantons of the Red River Delta, and elsewhere in Tonkin. In 1923 about 4,000 labourers under contract made the journey south; by 1928 the number had increased to 18,000.[37]

Until the late 1920s, there was no regulation of labour recruitment, although the Labour Codes of 1910 and 1918 limited voluntary contracts to three years, the working day to ten hours, and required paid overtime. There were to be rest days and observance of religious holidays. Planters recruited workers through agents who subcontracted the task to *cais*, who were familiar with local conditions and language, and in contact with village heads and landlords. Workers were threatened with *corvée* service and foreclosure if they did not sign indentures which bound them to plantation labour.[38] The *cais* misrepresented the conditions of plantation employment – including wage levels, repatriation rights, accommodation and food. They used alcohol and other drugs to help delude recruits, and also used press gangs to collect them.[39] This produced high desertion rates among contract workers, as high as ten per cent in 1927.

Plantation conditions were often appalling. The coolies were housed in rough barracks. The rice was of poor quality, wet and badly processed. Fish and meat were served rarely, and then were often rotten. Guard posts on the plantation perimeter kept coolies in, and intruders out. Desertion, sickness and death resulted in a very high labour turnover and an unwillingness to renew contracts.[40] But despite this, contract labour remained attractive to employers. The Labour Codes provided heavy penalties for breaches of work discipline. Absence from the plantation without excuse for 48 hours or more constituted desertion, and the law punished deserters with imprisonment (six to 60 days) and/or fines (16 to 20 francs).[41] Police and militia hunted down runaway coolies. During the 1920s thousands of deserters were returned to their plantations.[42] Many plantations resembled jails.[43]

In ironic contrast, French administrators were conscious of themselves as torch-bearers of the land of the Great Revolution. Governor General Georges Sarraut declared: 'Our native policy is the Declaration of the Rights of Man as interpreted by St. Vincent de Paul'.[44] But collusion between planters and the Administration sanctioned cruelty and denied coolies even the most elementary of human rights. By the mid-1920s the death rate amongst contract coolies on the rubber plantations of the 'red lands' was at least double the average for Cochinchina.[45]

The total outlay for recruiting the indentured labour force amounted to about seven million francs.[46] Coolies who died or were chronically ill were both expensive and numerous. In 1927, the proportion of coolies unfit for work was on average 12 per cent. Hospital cases numbered 265 per thousand, and the average mortality rate per thousand was 54.[47] The 1918 Code had required the planters to provide their workers with medical treatment, but the regulations were clearly ineffective.

After 1924 the *Institut Pasteur* advised the government to undertake a series of measures to combat malaria. In response, the Government drained swamps, constructed access roads and provided strong incentives for planters to build efficient hospitals. In October 1927, the Governor General issued detailed health regulations. Planters had to provide pure water and hot tea, distribute adequate supplies of quinine, supply vegetables as well as the mandatory rice ration, and issue boots and leggings to workers engaged on clearing. By 1927, the death rate among plantation workers was 5.4 per cent; by 1930 it had fallen to 2.32 per cent.[48]

The two greatest innovations of the new regulations were the establishment of the General Labour Inspectorate and the *pecule*. The *pecule* system required the plantation owner to withhold five per cent of each coolie's wages, add five per cent from their own funds, and bank the sum with the *caisse de pecule*, where it earned interest. Coolies who absconded, or were guilty of serious disciplinary offences, lost their *pecule*. Those who completed their contract period had savings to repatriate.

The last of the new series of labour regulations were promulgated in 1930. They were designed to dampen the mood of worker unrest, improve the general conditions for the bulk of workers and discipline agitators. In 1930, members of an insurrectionary group shot and killed Hervé Bazin, owner of the largest recruitment agency. His death marked a peak in campaigns against the recruitment of Tonkinese coolies in which both revolutionary groups and local employers took part.[49]

In the late 1920s the international price of rubber fell from 73 US cents per pound in 1925 to 22 cents by 1928, and to less than three cents four years later.[50] Throughout the 25 or so large plantations and among the more than 30,000 workers tensions mounted. The planters intensified the work process, reduced wages from four to three francs per day and cut rations. The number of beatings, fines, imprisonments and absconders all increased. Coolies worked without overtime up to 17 hours each day. If onerous quotas were not fulfilled, then wages and rations were withheld. To meet these quotas sometimes the unpaid labour of wives and children had to be mobilized.[51] Planters continued to flog, imprison workers, and use handcuffs, iron collars and chains. They faced resistance both spontaneous and organized.

Rather than let the rubber industry weather the storm unaided, the government provided loans and subsidies to planters to be able to produce more efficiently when prices recovered. This demonstrated the political influence – via the Indochina Lobby – of the planters and their French backers. The colonial state also helped to protect their stock holdings in rubber companies, exchanged as payment for land concessions.[52] The government also disbanded the Labour Inspectorate.

In Indochina, though trade unions were proscribed, protest took on not just an economic but a directly political character. Communist Party cadres began to organize insurrection. These cadres were often recruited and trained in the illegal unions of Saigon. In January 1930, coolies at Phu-rieng demonstrated for the release of a militant prisoner, and presented a list of industrial reforms. They demanded an eight-hour working day (including travelling time to and from work), the prohibition of assault by overseers, the ending of wage deductions, accident compensation and repatriation at the end of contract. Troops quelled the revolt. The leaders were arrested, tried and condemned to Paolo-Condor prison. In prison a militant and educated leadership cadre began to form.

There were uprisings on other plantations in the next few years and at least one union of agricultural workers was formed. The French arrested its leaders, sentencing them to 2–5 years' imprisonment, and forbidding them to return to their villages for ten years. Uprisings in the countryside were energized by political activity in the towns, where the Communist Party and other groups led strikes, and published revolutionary newspapers in collabouration with their international associates. French socialists and communists and some *colons* supported this radicalization. The largest social group that suffered during the depression was paradoxically not the plantation workers, but Vietnamese teachers and lower bureaucrats who lost their government employment. As these disaffected groups joined forces, the administration increased surveillance and prosecuted militants. With their hands full in Saigon (and particularly in Cholon), they believed (incorrectly) that the plantations were under control.

In the 1930s companies began to experiment with ways of securing a reliable supply of labour. The developmental work was now complete, and a different kind of flexible and skilled workforce was required. Accommodation and food rations were improved, women were encouraged to migrate south to join or accompany their men-folk, and to form family-based villages on land provided by the company administration. Savings from their *pecule* helped plantation workers establish communities, complete with agricultural plots, which were more attractive than the crowded villages in the North.

The new settlements provided plantation managers with a growing supply of 'free' labour which could be more reliable. Plantation owners on the smaller and older plantations closer to Saigon had been making use of free labour since the 1920s. Planters often complained that locals only worked when they wanted to, and were likely to walk off the job, because they had access to '*resources accessoires*', other sources of income from village work, or small plots of land.[53]

Between 1925 and 1935, over 10,000 coolies deserted: runaway coolies sometimes re-emerged as 'free' labourers. Others at the end of their contract simply stayed on without contract. Repatriation was not a general right until 1935, although some contracts drawn up previously did provide for it. From the early 1930s, the great majority of coolies signed on for another term. Coolies often reached the end of their term still in debt, and unable to pay their tax. They continued as coolies.

By the mid-1930s, the plantation owners increasingly offered work to wage labour. They paid a simple task rate and labourers were free also to employ their wives and children. Other managers offered both a morning and afternoon rate. Typically smaller plantations were worked on the basis of an eight-, or eight-and-a-half-hour day, with labourers paid 20 piastres for four hours in the morning and/or the same in the afternoon.[54] Workers lived on or nearby the plantation in villages with access to local markets, pagodas and churches.[55] By the end of the 1930s, most workers were 'local' people, but there was a sizeable minority which still identified itself as Tonkinese or Annamite.[56]

On bigger plantations, the largest importers of contract labour, free labourers were a smaller part of the workforce. But on some middle-sized plantations, they equalled or actually outnumbered the indentured coolies by 1937.[57] There were sound reasons why employers often found 'free' labour more attractive. Their actual daily rate of pay, though variable, was generally higher than the contract daily rate. For some plantations, so was their real cost, because the manager accorded them the 'advantages' of the indentured worker: rice, medical care and accommodation. But on others, they had none of these privileges and since both planters and the Labour Inspectorate agreed that these were worth about 15 piastres per day, 'free' labour's actual cost was lower.[58] Many planters thought so, and used the rates of free labour – determined by supply and demand – to argue for a reduction in the rates paid to indentured coolies.[59]

The working conditions and the payment of coolies became the subject of closer external scrutiny after 1936. The Popular Front won the French elections of that year. The Metropolitan Left had long criticized labour conditions in Indochina, as had the International Labour Office in Geneva. The new Government established the Guernot Commission to examine all aspects of French colonialism. Commissioner Jean Goudal, of the International Labour Office, was asked to report on labour conditions in Indochina, and recommended improvements. Goudal was part of a large French delegation which contained communists and socialists.

Goudal reported on attempts at 'civilizing native labour' and bringing their sense of responsibility to the level of European workers. He lamented that: 'the indigenous workers do not work as diligently as European workers'.[60] He supported 'the social and humanitarian plan which it is the duty of France to develop and extend in the territories it governs and administrates'.[61] Goudal focused on improving regulations and the labour code, more thorough inspections and reporting, and greater control over the Vietnamese *cais* and labour recruiters. He conceded that payments for plantation workers were low and intermittent, that saving was impossible and interest charges crippling.[62] He did suggest that the plantation managers' refusal to increase wages, or implement labour regulations, was responsible for the increasing unrest among plantation workers, and the success of communist agitation.

Less than a year later, the Popular Front Government collapsed, effectively ending French and international pressure for labour reform in Indochina. During the Japanese occupation, with the tacit acceptance of the Vichy government, the French colonial regime remained largely intact. The property rights of the plantation owners were protected. Key export commodities, especially rice, were diverted to the Japanese market, where they were paid for in Yen-based promissory notes which later proved worthless.

Throughout the war and beyond, the dual labour market – indentured and free – continued on the plantations. French ownership of the large plantations and the role of centralized finance capital continued. Labour conditions and production technology remained relatively constant. Neither the indentured nor 'free' labour was in a position to bargain collectively or withdraw its labour from exploitative employers. Many were wage labourers, but far from a self-conscious proletariat. Nevertheless, the plantation workers were transformed into a considerable political force through the organic associations linking them to urban workers, educated school teachers and public servants, to French and international revolutionary movements and to a battle hardened and disciplined leadership. Protest on the plantations was to become part of a revolutionary movement.

Northern Australia

The cattle industry in Northern Australia developed in the latter part of the nineteenth century in tropical lands alienated from the local Aboriginal population. The industry was export oriented. Capital investment was limited and the industry required large amounts of labour at certain times of the year. The industry was based on a few white owners and overseers but most of the labour was done by Aborigines. Employers and governments faced the problem of recruiting and motivating those whom they had recently dispossessed from the land and turning them into a workforce for an alien industry, by 1920 mostly owned by companies based in Britain. Accomplishing this task was possible because the process of conquest and subjugation had destroyed the economic basis of traditional Aboriginal societies, except in the remotest and most inhospitable areas.

Aborigines became dependent on rations provided by pastoralists and were forced to work and conform to obtain them. From the beginning, drugs, tobacco and alcohol were used to induce dependence. Payment in cash for labour was rare, except in Queensland, but by the 1920s a new Aboriginal work culture based on cattle had evolved in many places. Aborigines took on many specialist roles in areas such as droving and mustering, and women and children worked in and around homesteads where permanent camps were established. However, despite their dependence, Aborigines would walk off from time to time, sometimes to attend to spiritual duties and occasionally to protest about unfair treatment. Walkabout was most likely to occur just after the rainy season when abundant bush tucker was available. Until after the Second World War, such protests were usually confined to one station, were uncoordinated, without the backing of an industrial union and had no effect on the terms and conditions of Aboriginal employment.

Governments had begun to regulate the use of Aboriginal labour at the end of the nineteenth century, but in most areas the impact of this was slight. Discipline was largely left to individual bosses, violence was common and Aborigines had little recourse to the white justice system. The main support the state gave to the pastoralists was through the threat of exile from their land for Aborigines who deserted their employers and failed to work. In Western Australia, Aborigines were kept in chains and leg irons and transported to the south of the state. In Queensland, settlements such as Palm Island were used to discipline 'run-aways'. The importance of the land to Aborigines made this an especially severe punishment for failing to observe the work discipline required by the cattle industry.

In the 1920s, the plight of Aboriginal labour in the cattle industry became more widely known. The efforts of some observers such as clergy and mission staff began to make conditions known to the Australian public and ensured that international organizations such as the Anti-Slavery Society and even the emerging International Labour Office began to pay attention to Aboriginal labour.

The 1930s depression devastated the industry and put even more pressure on Aboriginal workers, but some signs of change began to emerge at this time. The North Australian Workers Union (NAWU) brought a case before the Commonwealth Arbitration Court seeking equal pay for Aborigines in the cattle industry. The Court refused the application. In urban areas, Aboriginal organizations began to develop and some members of the Communist Party took an interest in Aboriginal matters. There was a public outcry against police 'hunting parties' to punish Aborigines and a number of Royal Commissions and Enquiries about aspects of Aboriginal administration were undertaken, but on the pastoral frontier these had little impact.

Governments imposed minimal regulation, but even this was rarely enforced. In the Northern Territory, Aboriginal Ordinances in 1918 and 1933 prescribed a wage of five shillings per week, but in practice, few if any employers in the cattle industry were paying their Aboriginal employees wages as late as 1941. According to V. G. Carrington, whom the Commonwealth Government commissioned to report on the employment of Aborigines in 1945, only the right to quit distinguished the employment conditions of most Aborigines in the Northern Territory's cattle industry from those of slaves.[63] Not all could exercise that right. Some Aborigines did succeed in withdrawing their labour, but for others, walking off the job was practically impossible. It was always a very long way from the station to anywhere else. Employers organized against what a later Ordinance would describe as the 'enticement' of labour, and police cooperated with employers in returning runaways. Employers commonly enforced discipline on the job through violence, or threat of violence; they were particularly rough with those who tried to leave their employment during the busy season.[64]

From early 1942 however the Australian Army and the Royal Australian Air Force became alternative employers of Aborigines in much of the Northern Territory. Threat of invasion by the Japanese led to the hurried construction of airstrips and thousands of miles of road. The Air Force and the Army together employed more Aborigines than the cattle industry, mainly as labourers. They enjoyed the same food, clothing and shelter as their white counterparts. Moreover, both the Air Force and the Army paid wages in cash.[65]

The civilian administration of the Territory had all but collapsed after the Japanese bombed Darwin, and in 1942 neither Service paid too much attention to the Ordinances and Regulations, and for a while some even received the going rate for equivalent white labour. The soldiers and airmen, recruited from outside the Territory, worked alongside Aborigines without enforcing the prejudices of their pastoral employers.[66]

Aborigines did not forget their wartime experiences when the war ended. In Darwin, they went on strike in 1947, and again in 1950.[67] In 1949, the Administrator of the Territory noted that there had been, 'some unsettlement ... as a result of payment of wages by the Army ... frequently the natives will not work for an employer who does not pay wages'.[68]

It was because the Administration had anticipated this 'unsettlement', that it had commissioned V. G. Carrington to report on the working conditions of Aborigines. Carrington found many breaches of the Regulations, especially those relating to food, accommodation and hygiene. He recommended that these conditions be greatly improved, and that employers pay Aborigines a minimum wage, without the option of payment in kind. The rates he suggested were two pounds ten shillings per week for men over 21, and ten shillings a week for women.

The cattlemen objected, and it was not until 1947 that a conference between them and the Administration settled on a compromise, which was to pay Aboriginal stockmen with more than three years experience one pound a week, with keep. Even so, it was not until 1949 that the Government gazetted the necessary regulations. The Basic Wage which had to be paid as a minimum to every white adult male in the 'Top End' of the Northern Territory was then almost eight pounds per week, without keep.

The War had done more than 'unsettle' the Aborigines industrially. In unmeasurable but powerful ways it had influenced the attitude of Australians towards the subordination of a racial group. More Australians than ever before had had direct contact with Aborigines and a sense of equality had developed among wartime comrades. The Declaration of Human Rights and the trials of Nazis for war crimes they had justified on the basis of racial superiority strengthened the arguments of those who argued that Aborigines should make some real and immediate progress towards the attainment of full citizenship. One of these was Paul Hasluck, who became Minister for Territories in 1953.

At Hasluck's insistence, the Commonwealth Government repealed the Aboriginal Ordinance and replaced it with the Welfare Ordinance, 1953. The new Ordinance did not use the term 'Aboriginal'. It specified that those deemed to be 'in need of assistance' would be enrolled in a Register of Wards (more commonly known as the 'Stud Book'). This created a legally defined distinction between full-blood Aborigines, and those of mixed descent, who were automatically exempt from all legislation relating to Wards unless they were specifically declared to be subject to it.[69]

Complementing the Welfare Ordinance was the Wards' Employment

Ordinance of the same year. This Ordinance, and the Regulations made pursuant to it, determined the wages and working conditions of those Aborigines named in the Register, though the Ward's wage as set by the Regulations still compared very poorly with that of an adult male in the 'Top End' of the Territory.[70] As with the previous Ordinance, it empowered the Protector to bank the wages of the Aboriginal employees in their names, and release their savings to them on approval. Section 46 made it illegal for a person to 'entice or persuade a ward to leave his lawful employment'.[71]

These changes significantly advanced Territory Aborigines towards equal citizenship. They acquired the right to vote in Commonwealth and Territory elections, and unless they were nomadic, to take advantage of the full range of Commonwealth social services. The Government repealed the Welfare Ordinance in 1963, and removed restrictions placed on them by other legislation. In 1964, the Protector lost the right to acquire the wages of his Aboriginal wards and release money from their bank accounts at his discretion.

Aborigines had gained control over their wages, but they remained unable to bargain for them, or receive them according to the prevailing Award. That required the amendment or repeal of the Wards' Employment Ordinance, and that in turn, the Government decided, would have to wait on the result of the claim for variation of the Pastoral Award that the NAWU had brought before the Commonwealth Arbitration Commission.

The Commission said that it was impressed by the employers' evidence on work of equal value and recognized a risk of mass unemployment,[72] but it believed that the time had arrived when there had to be one industrial law for all Australians. It agreed to delete the words excepting Aborigines, but with effect only from the first pay period in December 1968. It suggested that in the intervening three years, the parties should confer and reach agreement on a plan to phase in equal pay.

Some Aborigines found three years too long to wait, and walked off two stations, leaving them without Aboriginal labour for the coming dry season. The third walk-off, at Wave Hill, attracted wide support from the Communist Party and unions in the Southern states, and television coverage made it world famous. When they walked off Wave Hill Station, the Gurindji people camped on traditional tribal land, and claimed it back from 'the 'Bestey (Vestey) mob' that operated the Station.[73] Although their dispute began over pay, it had by July 1966 broadened to one over control of land, and the Gurindjis determined to remain where they were until their land claim was settled.

The Gurindjis' decision was reinforced by the dispute between the cattlemen, the unions and the Administration over the phasing in of the Commission's decision. The NAWU rejected the first offer by the employers, but it was reluctant to extend the strike because of the costs involved in supporting the strikers. The parties reached agreement in September 1966 on a complicated wage structure based on the evaluation of the degree of skill of the employees, and finally full Award rates applied to all employees from the first pay period in December 1968.

It is difficult, if not impossible, to be precise about the effect that the payment of Award rates had on the employment of Aborigines in the cattle industry, but by the mid-1970s, the trend towards the permanent 'disemployment' of Aborigines in the cattle industry was unmistakable.[74] Its causes lay not in the simple substitution of white for black labour but in a massive investment in improving the technology of the industry. This investment programme was not aimed only at reducing the need for Aboriginal labour. In giving evidence to the Arbitration Commission in 1965, Mr R. T. Schmidt, an Executive Committee member of the Northern Territory Pastoral Lessees' Association, had said, 'No, I would not say we were intending to switch in any way, but we are probably working towards a stage where we employ a minimum of any type of labour . . . '[75]

Conclusion

In each of the industries, protest evolved from individual acts of desertion, self-harm or isolated assaults or over murder of overseers and managers, to collective action. The trigger for this was the linking of individual grievances to emerging nationalist and anti-racist sentiments. This involved not so much a conscious ideology as identification with a mythical belief. In Assam, in 1920, it was the myth of the simple native village life that the National Congress and especially Mahatma Gandhi preached to the millions. In the Northern Territory in 1965, the Gurindjis and others walked off from their employment to seek return of their traditional land, and a recreation of the life that it had once sustained. In Indochina, myth was more directly linked with ideology. Mythology favoured returning to the northern village or creating a new one in the South, but village traditions, especially from Annam, supplied a tradition of revolt against corrupt and oppressive governments. An increasingly active Communist Party expounded an ideology that not only explained the motives of the exploiters, but promised victory to the organized oppressed. It also provided schooling in the tactics of revolt, and in the use of the industrial and political strike as a liberating weapon.

In all three countries, governments reacted in similar ways to the labourers' protests, although their reactions differed in degree. All condoned the private and violent repression exercised by employers and managers. All reinforced employers' authority by police action; in Indochina and Assam, governments resorted to military intervention. But it is too simple to say that the governments reinforced the authority of the employers absolutely and on all occasions. The governments had purposes of their own, and their policies took account of broader and longer-term concerns than the generation of maximum profit in the current year.

In Indochina and Assam, provincial governments had to put into practice the policies and strategies of the home governments of which they were the colonial expression. The Governor of Indochina had to ensure that the plantations of his country supplied the industry of metropolitan France with the rubber it needed. The Government was responsible for seeing that the management of plantations ensured reliable long-term production of strategic commodities, not simply instant profits for shareholders. There were other concerns that all three governments had to consider. From the 1920s, international agencies took an increasing interest in slavery and 'unfree' labour, and governments protected themselves by drawing up detailed codes for the conduct of labour relations between labourers and the employers, and for the housing and feeding of the former. Their compromise with plantation and cattle station owners and managers was that there would be no serious attempt to enforce the regulations so made.

But in both Indochina and Australia, governments had to make some attempts to check *laissez-faire* operation: in Indochina sooner, in Australia later. In Indochina, the blindness of the planters to their own longer-term interests drove the Governor to attempt to enforce a wage rise, and the Popular Front government sought the proper implementation of the labour codes. In Australia, 30 years later, the Arbitration Commission reflected a significant shift in public opinion when it ordered that Aborigines in the cattle industry be paid the same wages as whites.

In Indochina, the planters simply ignored the Governor, relying on their Paris lobby to allow them to wait out time until the Popular Front government fell. In Australia, no such tactic was available to the cattle owners, but their response was more decisive: they substituted capital infrastructure for labour so effectively that the cattle industry within a few years was employing only a small fraction of the labour it had employed before the Equal Pay judgement.

The similarity in the management styles of plantation owners and cattle station companies stemmed from the economies of their industries. All of them operated in export industries in which world commodity prices oscillated quite widely. All of them were responsible to shareholders who expected high profit to compensate for the risks attached to their colonial investment. Their profits were derived from the companies' ability to hold down the price of labour in labour-intensive industries whose technologies did not change significantly. In this they were abetted by governments that, despite their own concerns, had to ensure the continuation of investment.

Notes

* The authors would like to thank the Australian Research Council for funding this project.
1 Sir Henry Cotton, *New India* (London: Kegan Paul, 1907), p. 28 and *passim.* Cotton was Chief Commissioner of Assam.
2 D. V. Regi, *Report on an Enquiry into Conditions of Labour in Plantations in India* (Government of India, New Delhi 1946), p. 54.

3 Regi, *Report on an Enquiry*, p. 56.
4 Government of Assam, *Act No 11*, assented to 11 September 1908, Government of Assam, *Resolution on Immigrant Labour in Assam*, Shilling, 1908, cited in *International Labour Review*, V (1928), p. 603.
5 P. Griffiths, *A History of the Indian Tea Industry* (London: Weidenfeld & Nicholson, 1967), p.101.
6 M. A. B. Siddique, *Evolution of Land Grants and Labour Policy of Governments*, (New Delhi: South Asia Publishers, 1990), p. 159.
7 Ibid. p. 171.
8 Ibid. p. 173.
9 Report of the Assam Labour Enquiry Committee, 1921/22, quoted in ibid. p. 175.
10 Siddique, *Evolution of Land Grants*, p. 176.
11 Report of the Royal Commission on Labour in India, p. 372, in *British Parliamentary Papers*, Vol. XI, London, 1931.
12 Siddique, *Evolution of Land Grants*, p. 161.
13 Ibid. p. 176.
14 Regi, *Report on an Enquiry*, p. 28.
15 Ibid. p. 28.
16 Ibid. p. 29.
17 Ibid. p. 29.
18 C. Revri, *The Indian Trade Union Movement* (New Delhi: Orient Longman, 1972), p. 236.
19 Regi, *Report of an Enquiry*, p. 71.
20 Ibid. p. 71.
21 Ibid. p. 56.
22 Ibid. p. 51.
23 Ibid. p. 72.
24 Ibid. p. 30.
25 Legislative Assembly of Assam, *Questions and Answers*, 18 February 1936, p. 987.
26 Ibid. p. 986.
27 Paul Doumer, *L'Indochine Française* (Paris: Vuibert, 1905), p. 287.
28 Doumer, *L'Indochine Française*; Pierre Gourou, *The Tropical World* (London: Longmans, 1966), pp. 118–27.
29 Doumer, *L'Indochine Française*, p. 287ff.
30 Gouchoc, NV. 904, Les Impôts Directs . . . 1930, Vietnamese Archives Number Two, Ho Chi Minh City.
31 Ngo Vinh Long, *Before the Revolution: The Vietnamese Peasants Under the French* (Cambridge, Mass: MIT Press, 1973), pp. 63ff.
32 Martin J. Murray, *The Development of Capitalism in Colonial Indochina 1870–1940*, (Berkeley: University of California Press, 1980), p. 227.
33 Ibid. p. 162.
34 Ibid.
35 Charles Robequain, *The Economic Development of French Indo-China* (Oxford University Press, New York 1944), p. 213.
36 Jean Goudal, *Labour Conditions in Indo-China* (Geneva: International Labour Office, 1938), p. 86.
37 Corvée service was forced labour. The predecessors of the French had used it for the construction and maintenance of public works like dykes and roads. It was 'rachetable', i.e. it could be bought out in money.
38 Goudal, ibid. p. 151.
39 Bruno Lasker, *Human Bondage in Southest Asia* (Chapel Hill, Westport: University of North Carolina Press, 1950), p. 258.
40 Murray, *Development of Capitalism*, p. 240.

41 E. Delamarre, *L'Emigration et l'immigration Chinois ouvrière en Indochine* (Hanoi: IDEO, 1931), p. 27.
42 Robequain, *Economic Development*, pp. 217, 189; and Goudal, Ibid. p. 94.
43 Interview with Coolies, Dong-Phu, 15 January 2000.
44 Goudal, Ibid. p. 86, Virgninia Thompson claims it was four to five times as high – see V. Thompson, *French Indo-China* (New York: Octagon Books, 1968), p. 155.
45 Thompson, *French Indo-China*, p. 90.
46 Goudal, Ibid. p. 90.
47 Ibid.
48 Delamarre, *L'Emigration et l'immigration*, pp. 8–13.
49 Ibid.
50 See Murray, *Development of Capitalism*, pp. 261–3.
51 Ibid. pp. 291–2.
52 P. Brocheux, 'The State and the 1930s Depression in French Indo-China', in P. Boomgaraard and I. Brown (eds), *Weathering the Storm: The Economies of Southeast Asia in the 1930s Depression* (Singapore: ISEAS, 2000), p. 254.
53 Gouchoc, Commission on Labour, 29 May, 1937 – Vietnamese Archives No. 2, Ho Chi Minh City (hereafter VA.2).
54 Gouchoc, HSTU AS/253 (18) Rapports des Inspections des Plantations par l'Inspectrice feminine, VA.2.
55 Ibid.
56 Ibid.
57 Gouchoc, H.S. III AS/253 (18) Reports of Inspection of Plantations, VA.2.
58 Gouchoc, I.B. 23/09/091 (9), Return for 1926 of concessions of more than 50 hectares, January 1927; do HSA202, Commission on Labour, 29 May, 1937, VA.2.
59 Gouchoc, IIA 45/494 (6) Rapport sur la Régime de la Main d'oeuvre Enga_ee, 1937, VA.2.
60 Goudal, *Labour Conditions*, p. 130.
61 Ibid. p. 156.
62 Ibid. p. 148.
63 V. G. Carrington to Administrator, 10 October 1945, in Bovril Australian Estate Records, File 42/14/1, Australian National University Archives of Business and Labour, Canberra.
64 L. A. Riddett, *Kine, Kin and Country: The Victoria River District of the Northern Territory, 1911–1966* (Darwin: Australian National University, North Australia Research Unit, 1990), p. 90.
65 For a discussion of the employment of Aborigines in the Second World War, see R. A. Hall, *The Black Diggers* (Sydney: Allen & Unwin 1989), chs. 7–8.
66 E. M. Andrews, *A History of the Department of Defence*, (Melbourne: Oxford University Press, 2001), ch. 5.
67 Department of Aboriginal Affairs, File F1 1958/1710, Australian Archives, Darwin.
68 Department of Aboriginal Affairs, File F1 1958/1710 Document 7 February, 1949 Australian Archives, Darwin.
69 Welfare Ordinance 1953–60, *Commonwealth Government Gazette* (1960), p. 2307ff.
70 *Year Book Australia*, 38 (1951), p. 431. The 'Top End' rate, set on 1 November 1949, was seven pounds nineteen shillings and nine pence.
71 Wards' Employment Ordinance, 1953–59, *Commonwealth Government Gazette* (1959), p. 2271ff. Section 40 provided a penalty of 50 pounds.
72 Statement by Kerr QC for the employers, C. No. 830, transcript, pp. 144–71, Foyer Library, University of Queensland, Brisbane.

73 Frank Hardy, *The Unlucky Australians* (Melbourne: Pan Books, 1968), p. 151ff.
74 For statistics on Aboriginal unemployment, see 'Report of the Committee to Review the Situation of Aborigines on Pastoral Properties in the Northern Territory', (the 'Gibb Report') Commonwealth Parliamentary Papers, 1971.
75 Transcript C. No. 830, p. 863. See also Kerr QC, File 1, p. 64 of transcript, Fryer Library, University of Queensland, Brisbane.

Index

Abel, Arie 16
Aborigines 5, 7, 105–9
accommodation 8, 75–9
African slave protest: Imperial Madagascar 51–5
age profile 1
Amina 36
Annet, Armand 62, 64, 65
anti-*fanompoana* protest 56–7
Anti-Slavery Society 106
Armanet 41, 44
Assam 7, 96–9
attacks 12
Australia: cattle industry 5, 7, 105–9
Australian Army 106
Awes 35–6

Barile, Pietro 26, 27
'Bastaard' community 11
Bazin, Hervé 8, 102
Bédier, Benjamin 46
Boiteau, Pierre 66
Bokkeveld 15–16
brigands 57–8
Britanno-Merino alliance 49
buinda ritual 30

Caledon Code (1809) 17
Cape Colony: flight 6–7, 10–12; resistance 10–12; revolts 13–19
Cape Hangklip 11
Carrington, V. G. 106, 107
cattle industry 105–9
Cayla, Léon 62
Christianity 4–5, 53
Ciret 41, 43, 44
Ciret, Paulin 45
'closed' slave systems 1
Communist ideology 5, 109

Communist Party 102–3
community solidarity 4
Comoro Islands 40
concessions: Mayotta 41–3; Somalia 25
coolies 97–9, 101–5
Cooper, Frederick 67
'Co-Prosperity Sphere' 86–7
creolization 12
Cultuurstelsel system (System of Cultivations) 3, 6, 70–1, 73, 77–8

Darwin 107
de Campher, Petrus Josephus 16
desertion *see* flight
De Vecchi, Paolo 25
De Zuid-Afrikaan 16
Doumer, Paul 99–100
drosters (escapees) 11–12
Dupérier, Armand 44
Dutch East India Company (VOC) 70

eastern Cape revolt 18–19
Elson, R. E. 74, 77–8
emancipation 18
escape *see* flight
escapees *(drosters)* 11–12

Fairbairn, John 16
fanompoana 50–1, 56–7, 61–2
Feeley-Harnik, Gillian 61
flight 6–7; Cape Colony 11–12; Gosha area 31; Imperial Madagascar 57–8; Java 74, 88–91; Vietnam 103
forced labour: Java 71–3; Mayotta 43–4; Zigula communities 24–9, 37
forced marriage 29–31, 38
'free' labour 103–4
French Indochina: flight 7; revenge 8; *see also* Vietnam

Galant (van der Caap) 15–16
Gallas, Joseph 45
gender issues 16
gender profile 1
Gevrey, Auguste 46
ghosts 89–90
gold mines 54, 57
Gosha area *see* Zigula communities
go-slow tactics 7, 31, 74–5
Goudal, Jean 104
'Greater East Asia Co-Prosperity Sphere'
     86–7
Guernot Commission 104
Gurindji people 108

Hallez, Theodore 45
Harris, Karen 14
Hasluck, Paul 107
hierarchy 1–2
Hottentots 16, 17
Hou-den-Bek farm 14–15

ideologies: Communist 5, 109;
     revolutionary 4–5
Imperial Madagascar: accommodation 8;
     African slave protest 51–5; anti-
     fanompoana protest 56–7; the army 50,
     51, 56; Christianity 4–5, 53; economy
     49–51; flight 6, 57–8; forced labour
     50–1; go-slows and strikes 7, 54;
     hierarchy 1–2; Malagasy slave protest
     55; political protest 57–8; revolts 4, 54;
     self-mutilation 6, 56; slaves 50
inboekstelsel (indenture) 17
indenture 17, 96–7
Indramayu 88–9
industrial action *see* strikes
International Labour Office 106
Institut Pasteur 101
Italian government 25
Italian marriage 29–31, 33, 37
Italian Somaliland: flight 7; revenge 8; *see
     also* Zigula communities

Jager, Dirk 16
Japanese occupation: of Java 3–4, 6–7,
     82–3, 85–93; of Vietnam 104
Java: accommodation 8, 75–9;
     economy (1929-1942) 83–5; flight
     6–7, 74; forced labour 71–3; go-slow
     tactics 7, 74–5; Japanese occupation
     3–4, 6–7, 82–3, 85–93; political
     economy 75–9; population 76–7;
     resistance 73–5, 87–90; revenge 8, 93;

revolts 3–4, 73–5; rice 84–5; servile
     labour 69–70

Kajendo Mganga, Mame 26
Kat River Settlement 18
Keray, Mame 29
Khoi 16, 17–18
Koussou, Bakari 45
Kutukira, Mame 30

labour mobilization 85–7, 90–1
labour recruitment 100–1
land claims 108–9
Launay, Buhot de 63–4
looting 13, 14
Lower River Juba region *see* Zigula
     communities
Luhizo Matua, Mze 31–2, 33–4

Madagascar: forced labour 61–7; resistance
     65–6; *see also* Imperial Madagascar
Maiange Chipande, Mze 8, 33–4
Malagasy slave protest: Imperial
     Madagascar 55
malaria 101
Mamadi Mgaia, Mze 32
Margherita 30
maroonage 6, 7
maroon communities 11
Mascarene islands 1
Master and Servant Ordinance (1841) 18
Mauritius 13, 40, 49
Mayotta: 1841 treaty 40, 41; concessions
     41–3, 46–7; forced labour 43–4;
     plantations 47; revolt 2–3, 44–7;
     slavery 40–1
Mberwa Sugini, Mze 32
Menalamba revolt 58
Merina Empire 49–50
migration 65–6, 91–2; *see also* flight
Mnongerwa, Mame Nthukano 30
Mois 100
Mosambika revolt 54–5
Mustofa, Kiai Zainal 87–8

Nam Po Ko 45
North Australia Workers Union (NAWU)
     106
Northern Australia: cattle industry 105–9
Noyce, Sir Frank 99
Nthukano Mnongerwa, Mame 29, 30

Onor, Romolo 25
Oorlam community 11

'open' slave systems 1

Passot, Pierre 44
Paulo-Condor prison 102
pecule system 102
petitioning 5
plantations 2–3, 7, 43, 46, 47, 96–9,
    100–5
Popular Front Government 104, 110
population: Java 76–7
porterage system 54
Pramoedya Ananta Toer 91–2
protests: Imperial Madagascar 51–8

Rabearimanana, Lucile 62
Radama I 56
Rainilaiarivony 54
ramanenjana 53
Randriamaro, Roland 66
Ratrematsialonina, Dox F. 61–2, 66
rebellions: Java 87–9
religion: impact of 1; *see also* Christianity
resistance: Aborigines 105, 106, 107,
    108–9; Imperial Madagascar 51–8; Java
    73–5, 87–90; Vietnam 102–3; Zigula
    communities 31–4, 37–8
Réunion 40
revenge 8
revolts: general 2–4; Java 73–5, 87–9;
    Vietnam 102–3
romusho forced labour regime: revenge 8;
    and revolts 3–4
Ross, Robert 11
Royal Australian Air Force 106
rubber plantations 100–5

Saigon 100, 103
San 17
Sarraut, Georges 101
Schmidt, R. T. 109
Scully, Pamela 16
self-mutilation 6, 56, 97
slavery: Mayotta 40–1
slave systems 1
Smith, Sir Harry 19
Socialist ideologies 5
social structures 1–2
soddon 26–7
Sohier de Vaucouleur, Léopold Joseph 45
Sohier de Vaucouleur plantation 43, 46
Somalia 4, 24; *see also* Zigula
    communities

South Africa: revolts 3; *see also* Cape Colony
South African Commercial Advertiser 16
Squatting Ordinance 19
Statistical Survey (*Statistiek Opname*):
    Indies Government 76–7
status 1–2
Stellenbosch 12
strikes 7, 31–2, 97–9, 107, 108
sugar production: Java 69–79
supernatural beings 88–9
Supriyadi 88
Suret-Canal, Jean 63

Tan Makala 82–3
taxation 100
tea plantations 7, 96–9
Tonkin 100
Toudic, Marcel 46
trade unions 98–9, 102–3
Trieng 100
Tygerberg march 13–14

unfree labour 1–2, 69–70
unions 98–9, 102–3, 106
uprisings *see* revolts

van der Caap, Abraham 13, 14
van der Caap, Galant 15–16
van der Spuy, Patricia 16
van Mauritius, Louis 13–14
Vérand, André César 44, 45, 46
Vichy regime: Madagascar 61–7
Vietnam 6, 99–105; *see also* French
    Indochina
Vignerie, Ernest 46
violence 82
VOC (Dutch East India Company) 70

WaGosh *see* Zigula communities
walkabouts 7, 105
walk-offs 108
Wave Hill walk-off 108
Welfare Ordinance 107–8
women: negative forms of resistance 5–6

Xhosa 17, 18

Zanj revolt 2
Zigula communities: attitudes 35–7;
    flight 31; forced labour 24–9, 37;
    forced marriage 29–31, 38; resistance
    31–4, 37–8; solidarity 4